WRITERS AND THEIR WORK

ISOBEL ARMSTRONG
General Editor

GEOFFREY HILL

D1584870

C333773243

GEOFFREY HILL

GEOFFREY HILL

Andrew Michael Roberts

NORTHCOTE

BRITISH
COUNCIL

© Copyright 2004 by Andrew Michael Roberts

First published in 2004 by Northcote House Publishers Ltd, Horndon, Tavistock, Devon, PL19 9NQ, United Kingdom.
Tel: +44 (01822) 810066. Fax: +44 (01822) 810034.

British Library Cataloguing-in-Publication Data
A catalogue record for this book is available from the British Library

ISBN 0-7463-1018-8 hardback
ISBN 0-7463-0879-5 paperback

Typeset by TW Typesetting, Plymouth, Devon
Printed and bound in the United Kingdom by
Athenaeum Press Ltd., Gateshead, Tyne & Wear

To the memory of my father, Patrick Roberts

Contents

Acknowledgements

I would like to thank all those whose comments and insights have helped me in my reading of Geoffrey Hill's poetry, notably Martin Dodsworth, Peter Easingwood, Philip Horne, Stephen James, Sally Kilmister, Elizabeth Maslen, Stephen Matthews, Christopher Ricks and Peter Robinson. Especial thanks go to Isobel Armstrong, Stephen Matthews and Stephen James for their advice on drafts of this book and to Sally Kilmister for support, advice and numerous insights into Hill's work. Tom Healy kindly suggested that I undertake this project. Some passages in chapter 3 rework material previously published in *Essays in Criticism*, and I am grateful to the editors and to Oxford University Press for permission to reuse this material. Particular thanks are due to Geoffrey Hill and to Christopher Carduff of Counterpoint Press for facilitating the permissions process and to Zelda Turner of Penguin Books for providing an advance copy of *The Orchards of Syon*.

Excerpts from *Canaan* by Geoffrey Hill (Penguin Books and Houghton Mifflin Company, 1996). Copyright © 1996 by Geoffrey Hill. Reprinted by permission of Penguin Books Ltd and Houghton Mifflin Company. All rights reserved.

Excerpts from *The Triumph of Love* by Geoffrey Hill (Houghton Mifflin Company and Penguin Books, 1998). Copyright © 1998 by Geoffrey Hill. Reprinted by permission of Houghton Mifflin Company and Penguin Books Ltd. All rights reserved.

Excerpts from *Speech! Speech!* by Geoffrey Hill (Counterpoint Press, 2000, and Viking, 2001). Copyright © 2000 and 2001 by Geoffrey Hill. Reprinted by permission of Counterpoint Press and Penguin Books Ltd. All rights reserved.

Excerpts from *The Orchards of Syon* by Geoffrey Hill (Counterpoint Press and Penguin Books, 2002). Copyright © 2002 by Geoffrey Hill. Reprinted by permission of Counterpoint Press and Penguin Books Ltd. All rights reserved.

Excerpts from 'The Tollund Man', from *Wintering Out* by Seamus Heaney (Faber and Faber, 1972). Copyright © 1972 by Seamus Heaney. Reprinted by permission of the author, Faber and Faber Ltd and Farrar, Straus and Giroux, LLC.

Excerpts from 'East Coker', 'Little Gidding' and 'The Dry Salvages', from *Four Quartets* by T. S. Eliot. Copyright © 1942 by T. S. Eliot. Reprinted by permission of the estate of the author, Faber and Faber Ltd and Harcourt, Inc.

Excerpts from Paul Celan, *Selected Poems*, translated by Michael Hamburger. Copyright © 1988 by Michael Hamburger. Reprinted by permission of Penguin Books Ltd.

Biographical Outline

1932	Born in Bromsgrove, Worcestershire, England, on 18 June.
1936	Hill family move to the nearby village of Fairfield, where Hill's father becomes village police constable, and Hill attends the Fairfield Junior School.
1942–50	Attends County High School, Bromsgrove.
1950–53	Attends Keble College, Oxford, graduating with a first-class degree in English.
1952	Publishes a pamphlet of poems with the Oxford-based Fantasy Press.
1954	Becomes lecturer in English at the University of Leeds, where he teaches until 1980.
1956	Marries Nancy Whittaker.
1959	*For the Unfallen* published.
1959–60	Visiting Lecturer, University of Michigan, USA.
1961	Death of Hill's mother, Hilda Beatrice Hill. Receives Gregory Award for *For the Unfallen*.
1964	*Preghiere* (pamphlet of eight poems) published in Leeds.
1967	Visiting Lecturer, University of Ibadan, Nigeria.
1968	*King Log* published.
1969	Receives Hawthornden prize for *King Log*.
1970	Receives Geoffrey Faber memorial prize for *King Log*.
1971	*Mercian Hymns* published and awarded Alice Hunt Bartlett Award. Receives Whitbread Award and Royal Society of Literature Award.
1972	Becomes Fellow of the Royal Society of Literature.

1975	*Somewhere is Such a Kingdom* published in America.
1977	Becomes Professor at the University of Leeds.
1978	*Tenebrae* published. Hill's version of Ibsen's *Brand* published, and staged at the National Theatre in London.
1979	Death of Hill's father, William George Hill. Receives Duff Cooper Memorial Prize for *Tenebrae*.
1980	Holds Churchill Fellowship, University of Bristol.
1981	Moves from Leeds to Cambridge, as University Lecturer in English and Fellow of Emmanuel College. Made Honorary Fellow of Keble College, Oxford.
1983	*The Mystery of the Charity of Charles Péguy* published. Hill's first marriage dissolved. Receives American Academy Russell Loines Award.
1984	*The Lords of Limit* published.
1985	*Collected Poems* published. Receives Ingram Merrill Foundation Award in Literature. Awarded DLitt, University of Leeds.
1986	Delivers Clark Lectures at Cambridge, later published as *The Enemy's Country*.
1987	Marries Alice Goodman.
1988	Moves to America to become Professor of Literature and Religion at Boston University.
1991	*The Enemy's Country* published.
1994	*New and Collected Poems* published in America.
1996	*Canaan* published. Becomes Fellow of the American Academy of Arts and Sciences.
1998	Becomes co-director of newly founded Editorial Institute in Boston. *The Triumph of Love* published.
2000	*Speech! Speech!* published.
2002	*Orchards of Syon* published.

Abbreviations and References

Works by Geoffrey Hill

BF	Interview with Hermione Lee, *Book Four*, 2 October 1985, Channel Four television
C	*Canaan* (Harmondsworth: Penguin, 1996)
CP	*Collected Poems* (Harmondsworth: Penguin, 1985)
EC	*The Enemy's Country: Words, Contexture, and Other Circumstances of Language* (Oxford: Clarendon Press, 1991)
FU	*For the Unfallen* (London: André Deutsch, 1959)
KL	*King Log* (London: André Deutsch, 1968)
LL	*The Lords of Limit: Essays on Literature and Ideas* (London: André Deutsch, 1984)
M	*The Mystery of the Charity of Charles Péguy* (London: Agenda Editions and André Deutsch, 1983) (numbers in citations refer to section and stanza numbers)
MH	*Mercian Hymns* (London: André Deutsch, 1971) (numbers in citations refer to hymn numbers)
NS	'Under Judgment': interview with Blake Morrison, *New Statesman*, 8 February 1980, 212–14
OS	*The Orchards of Syon* (Washington, DC: Counterpoint, 2002) (numbers in citations refer to section numbers)
PR	'The Art of Poetry LXX', Geoffrey Hill interviewed by Carl Phillips, *Paris Review*, 154 (Spring 2000), 272–99
S	*A Sermon Delivered at Great St Mary's University Church*, Cambridge, 8 May 1983
SS	*Speech! Speech!* (Washington, DC: Counterpoint, 2000) (numbers in citations refer to section numbers)
T	*Tenebrae* (London: André Deutsch, 1978)

TL   *The Triumph of Love* (Harmondsworth: Penguin, 1999) (numbers in citations refer to section numbers)

VP   Interview with John Haffenden, *Quarto*, 15 (March 1981), 19–22, reprinted in *Viewpoints: Poets in Conversation with John Haffenden* (London: Faber and Faber, 1981), 76–99

Other works

GH   Peter Robinson, ed., *Geoffrey Hill: Essays on his Work* (Milton Keynes: Open University Press, 1985)

FP   Christopher Ricks, *The Force of Poetry* (1984; repr. Oxford: Oxford University Press, 1987)

OED   *The Oxford English Dictionary*, 2nd edition (Oxford: Clarendon Press, 1989)

All biblical references are to the King James Authorized Version, unless otherwise indicated.

Note on Text

Hill's *Collected Poems* (1985) includes the complete texts of *For the Unfallen, King Log, Mercian Hymns, Tenebrae* and *The Mystery of the Charity of Charles Péguy*, with a very small number of minor revisions. These revisions have been incorporated into quotations, so that quotations from these volumes use the text as it appears in *Collected Poems*.

Introduction

Geoffrey Hill occupies a unique position in contemporary British poetry. Regarded by many, notably by many of his fellow poets, as a major writer, even as the greatest poet of his time, he has nevertheless not received the popular acclaim or wide readership of his contemporaries Ted Hughes and Seamus Heaney, and nor does he fit into any of the groupings by which poets are often identified. Even such a broad distinction as 'mainstream' versus 'alternative' poetries fails to accommodate Hill's resolute distinctiveness. Certainly one can find points of imaginative connection between Hill and his contemporaries, such as the fascination with landscape as record and symbol of the past which he shares with Heaney. By and large, though, the literary context for Hill's work seems to lie with British, American and European poets of earlier generations, such as T. S. Eliot, Ezra Pound, Basil Bunting, David Jones, Paul Celan, Osip Mandelstam, Charles Péguy, Allan Tate and Richard Eberhart; and with English poets of earlier centuries, such as Wordsworth, Coleridge, Donne and Herbert. Similarly, the intellectual context of his work is found less in contemporary thinkers than in the wide range of philosophical, theological and political writers of the past whom Hill discusses in his essays and frequently alludes to in his poetry. However, one of his recent volumes of poetry, *Speech! Speech!*, makes far greater allusion to contemporary culture, even if Hill's relationship to that culture remains characterized by principled resistance and an inclination to 'swim up against the stream' (*LL* 15). He is resolute in his insistence on the importance of the past, of individual and collective memory, to any real understanding of the present.

1

If this makes Hill sound a somewhat stern and forbidding figure, then it is certainly true that his manner in interviews and readings has been generally uncompromising (though less so in recent years) and that his work is often felt to be 'difficult'. His poems don't yield up their meanings quickly, or on a single reading; they frequently make allusions to literary and other texts, including relatively little-known ones (so that many readers will need to make use of reference works to help them); in style and syntactical structure they are highly condensed and ambiguous, and can pose a challenge to the reader's powers of interpretation and understanding. Hill has strongly defended such features of his poetry, arguing that 'one has to learn to read any real poem . . . a real poem does not just sit there ingratiating itself with you' (*BF*). However, the unrivalled rhetorical and musical power of Hill's poetry makes it immediately compelling, even before it is fully understood, and its density of meaning also prepares the way for moments of great clarity and lyrical beauty, and for images or emotions which emerge with luminous intensity. Hill himself has more than once expressed his aspiration, or claim, to write a poetry which would be, in Milton's words, 'simple, sensuous and passionate'.[1] There is also an often underrated vein of humour in Hill's poetry, which has become more evident in his recent work.

Geoffrey Hill was born in 1932 in the small market town of Bromsgrove, Worcestershire, in the West Midlands of England, and from 1936 to 1952 his home was in the village of Fairfield, some three miles north of Bromsgrove. His father and paternal grandfather were policemen: his grandfather had risen through the ranks to become Deputy Chief Constable of Worcestershire, while his father became police constable in Fairfield when Hill was 3 years old. Hill's maternal grandmother had worked as an artisan in 'the traditional cottage-industry of nail making', and Hill (who was an only child) lived with her 'in her tiny cottage at the end of a row' (*VP* 76) on two occasions during his childhood when his mother was seriously ill. He has commented on his close attachment to his grandmother, and she is commemorated in *Mercian Hymns*, hymn XXV. His mother's family belonged to the Baptist Church, but his mother joined the Church of England when they moved to Fairfield, and Hill sang in the church choir between the ages of 7 and 18. He has described being awakened, at the age of 7 or 8, to the power and beauty of both music and poetry, the latter through reading William Palgrave's famous anthology, *The Golden Treasury*, which he received as a Sunday-School prize.[2] Hill was educated at the village school, and then at the County High School, Bromsgrove, where his poems in the school magazine showed early promise. He has commented that 'I have been a poet for as long as I can remember', and has recalled his avid reading of Oscar Williams's *Little Treasury of Modern Verse* which his father bought for him at the age of about 15, along with A. E. Housman's *Collected Poems* (*VP* 78).[3] The landscape of Worcestershire, and of the West Midlands generally, is of considerable importance to Hill, and figures notably in *Mercian Hymns* and *The Triumph of Love*. He has commented on his fellow feeling with Housman (born in Fairfield) for whom, like Hill, the hills of Shropshire represented a familiar but distant prospect (*VP* 79).

In 1950 Hill went up to Keble College, Oxford, to study English. On his own account he found studying at Oxford a somewhat lonely and unhappy experience, at least at first (*VP* 77), but during these years he formed lasting friendships with the poet and critic Donald Hall and the poet David Wright, and by the time of his 'Letter from Oxford' (1954) he was alluding to the enjoyable company of a group of young Oxford writers.[4] He achieved some early literary success, publishing poems and reviews in the Oxford literary magazine, *The Isis*, and a Fantasy Press pamphlet (1952) in his third year. He took a first-class degree (1953) and went on, in 1954, to lecture in English at the University of Leeds, where he became a professor in 1977. He married Nancy Whittaker in 1956 and has three sons and one daughter from this marriage, which was dissolved in 1983. Between 1953 and his first major volume of poetry (*For the Unfallen*, 1959) Hill published a number of poems in journals, and in 1955 had two poems read on the BBC Radio programme *New Verse*, as well as publishing an essay on the American poet Allen Tate.[5] At Leeds, Hill formed a friendship with the poet Jon Silkin, and during the 1960s Silkin's Northern House published a pamphlet of eight

Hill poems (*Preghiere*, 1964), while the journal *Stand* (which Silkin edited) published many of the poems which were to be collected in *King Log* (1968). In 1965 Hill first published in the poetry journal *Agenda*, which was to remain one of the most important outlets for his poetry and criticism. *Mercian Hymns* (1971), a sequence of prose poems, represented a new departure in his work. It was followed by an American collection of Hill's first four volumes, *Somewhere is Such a Kingdom: Poems 1952–1971* (1975). Christopher Ricks was an early champion of Hill's poetry, praising it in the *London Magazine* in 1964. Hill's critical work of the 1960s included essays on Ben Jonson, Keith Douglas, Jonathan Swift and Shakespeare, the latter two subsequently included in *The Lords of Limit* (1984), a volume which also collects two essays published in the 1970s and of particular interest for a reading of his own poetry: 'Poetry as "Menace" and "Atonement" ' (originally his inaugural lecture in the University of Leeds in 1977), and 'Redeeming the Time' (1973). In 1978 Hill published his next volume of poetry, *Tenebrae* and a version of Ibsen's play *Brand*, working from an existing translation; Hill's *Brand* was staged at the National Theatre in London in the same year.

During the years that he taught at Leeds, Hill also taught on secondment in the USA (as Visiting Lecturer, University of Michigan, 1959–60) and in Nigeria (as Visiting Lecturer, University of Ibadan, 1967). In 1981 he moved to the University of Cambridge, as a University Lecturer in English and Fellow of Emmanuel College. During his time at Cambridge Hill published the volume-length poem *The Mystery of the Charity of Charles Péguy* (1983) and *Collected Poems* (1985), which included the five individual volumes, plus three 'Hymns to Our Lady of Chartres'. 'Our Word is our Bond' (1983) was an important critical essay on Ezra Pound (included in *The Lords of Limit*), and in 1986 he delivered the Clark Lectures at Cambridge, published with revisions in 1991 as his second volume of critical essays, *The Enemy's Country*. In 1987 he married the opera librettist, Alice Goodman, with whom he has a daughter.

In 1988 he became Professor of Literature and Religion at Boston University in America and, since 1998, has also been co-director of the newly founded Editorial Institute at Boston. He has contributed a number of substantial articles to the *Times*

Literary Supplement, notably reviews of the second edition of the *Oxford English Dictionary* (1989), of two editions of the Bible (1989), and of *Early Responses to Hobbes* (1999); his recent critical work has included articles on T. S. Eliot and on 'Language, Suffering and Silence'.[6] *New and Collected Poems,* which included the contents of *Collected Poems* while adding new work later to be included in *Canaan,* was published in America in 1994. He now lives in Brookline, Massachusetts, but spends summers in England, where he has a cottage in Lancashire; the surrounding landscape of the Hodder valley is a significant presence in *The Orchards of Syon.* The continuing importance of his family and social background were stressed by Hill in a recent interview: 'Not a day passes without my thinking of the dead of my own family, and my pride in them, and my gratitude to them . . . I'm glad and proud of being born into the English working class' (*PR* 298). He has also described how, following his move to America, he began for the first time to receive chemical treatment for the 'chronic depression . . . accompanied by various exhausting obsessive-compulsive phobias', which had troubled him, whilst remaining undiagnosed, since late childhood (*PR* 288). This treatment, Hill has said, has transformed his life, so that since around 1992 he has felt happier and 'more at home in the world' than ever before (*PR* 289). The treatment is also one of the causes of a prolific creative spurt, which has led to the publication of four new volumes of poetry within six years (in contrast to the relatively long gaps between volumes earlier in his career): *Canaan* (1996), *The Triumph of Love* (1998), *Speech! Speech!* (2000) and *The Orchards of Syon* (2002).

1

Identity and Otherness

'What we call the writer's "distinctive voice" is a registering of different voices'

– Geoffrey Hill (*EC* 80)

'From the depths of the self we rise to a concurrence with
that which is not-self'

– Geoffrey Hill (*LL* 3)

Much contemporary poetry in the British Isles remains
dominated by a particular model of what a lyric poem is and
how it may be read. According to this model a poem
represents the voice of the poet (or of a 'persona' who closely
resembles the poet). This voice uses imagery, metaphor and
other resources of poetic language to describe his or her own
experience and evoke the physical world, and in this way the
poet reveals something of him or herself through memory,
reflection and interaction with the external environment. The
topic of the poem may be a place, an issue, or an event, but the
centre of the poem is the subjectivity of the poet, and his or her
thoughts and feelings, and the reader is invited to identify with
this subjectivity, whilst seeing the poem as a form of self-
revelation or self-expression on the part of the poet. The idea
of the centrality of the poet's consciousness has its roots in
Romantic lyric poetry, though the model as I have described it
represents a simplified misreading of Romanticism. The cult
of personality, the popularity of autobiography and the fascination with the confessional and the intimate have all played
their part in the dominance of this way of reading lyric
poetry. This model has often been criticized as limiting, and
much postmodernist, avant-garde and 'linguistically innova-

tive' poetry has avoided it entirely, displacing the poet's voice
with forms of narrative, with dramatic monologue or with
linguistic structures which avoid any direct representation of
an individual consciousness. Nevertheless, since the 1960s
many of the best-known poets in Britain and Ireland, from
Philip Larkin, through Sylvia Plath and Ted Hughes, up to
established writers still active in the twenty-first century, such
as Seamus Heaney, Tony Harrison, Eavan Boland and Douglas
Dunn, have written poems which can be read in terms of
self-expression, even if such a reading rarely does justice to
the richness of their work. Furthermore, the expressive
model implicitly underlies most discussion of poetry in the
media.

Throughout his poetic career, from the 1950s to the present,
Geoffrey Hill has consistently set his face against this model. A
recurrent theme of his rare but forceful comments on contemporary poetry has been his suspicion of personal or confessional poetry and his objection to the tendency to read poetry
as 'self-expression'. Early in his career, Hill aligned himself
with T. S. Eliot's famous assertion that poetry 'is not the
expression of personality, but an escape from personality'[1]
(while suggesting that 'transcendence' might be a better word
than 'escape') (VP 86–7) and remarked acerbically that 'my
true feelings coincide with the American poet Allen Tate's
beleaguered minority opinion that "self-expression" is a word
that "should be tarred and feathered" ' (S 1). However, in an
interview for the Paris Review, published in 2000, Hill signalled
a certain softening (though not abandonment) of this position,
describing as 'far too extremist' his own earlier view that 'a
total incompatibility of the objective and the subjective' meant
that successful poetry required 'the fullest possible objectifica-
tion of individual subjectivity'. He had come to believe, he told
the interviewer, that while a lot of weak poetry of the second
half of the twentieth century was based on 'a naive trust in the
unchallengeable authority of the authentic self', the answer to
this problem lay in 'self-knowledge and self-criticism' rather
than in 'the suppression of self' (PR 282–3). Thus Hill does not
deny any role for the poet's self. Rather he is resisting the
tendency to project superficial versions of the self; what he
called, in a 1987 interview, the 'commodity exploitation of

personality' (*VP* 87). He continues to assert the importance of this distinction in 2000: 'one is right to distrust the opinion that associates self and self-expression, as if the self-expression were ectoplasm emanating in a tenuous stream from the allegedly authentic self' (*PR* 283).

These views are clearly reflected in Hill's own poetry, the themes of which are predominantly historical, religious and ethical, and which, at least up until the late 1990s, addressed the lives of others far more often than it alluded (at least in any explicit way) to his own life. In much of Hill's poetry up to and including *Canaan* the word 'I' does not appear, or if it does it clearly refers to someone other than the poet. *Mercian Hymns* alludes to his childhood, while his recent long poems *The Triumph of Love, Speech! Speech!* and *The Orchards of Syon* for the first time include a significant level of direct allusion to his adult experience, but, prior to these recent volumes, there were few overt allusions to Hill's own life in his poetry. Few of his poems seem to describe a place or an experience and express feelings about it in any straightforward way. There is however a strong sense of 'voice' in his poems, because of their rhetorical power, the strength of indignation, sorrow, longing or scepticism that they convey, and the characteristic tonality of his style, the way in which he uses verbal density to achieve a certain hieratical authority. Yet the result is somehow not a personal voice: as Romana Huk puts it, 'any conventional performance of lyric expressivism becomes all but impossible in Hill's poems, which are much more frequently spoken in a strangely choral voice, even when the personal pronoun is present – as though culture itself were speaking'.[2] Nevertheless, selfhood, which Hill has described as 'more vital, recalcitrant, abiding, than self-expression' (*S* 2), does have a place in his work, notably in a series of poems and sequences of poems which articulate forms of relationship between self and other. Such others include: a child victim of the Nazis in 'September Song'; a fictional Spanish poet in 'The Songbook of Sebastian Arrurruz'; the historical but semi-legendary King Offa of Mercia in *Mercian Hymns*; major European poets of the twentieth century in *The Mystery of the Charity of Charles Péguy*, 'Scenes with Harlequins' and 'Two Chorale-Preludes'; hostile or comic-satirical voices in *The Triumph of Love*; a multitude of

8

competing discourses (many from the contemporary media) in *Speech! Speech!* In these works Hill explores a range of forms of self–other relation: identification across an unbridgeable gulf in 'September Song'; the ironical play of closeness and distance in 'The Songbook of Sebastian Arrurruz'; mutual exchange and reciprocity in *Mercian Hymns*; oblique mirroring in *The Mystery of the Charity of Charles Péguy*; challenge and vituperation in *The Triumph of Love*; humour, defiance, mockery and self-mockery in *Speech! Speech!* This first chapter examines Hill's strategies in these poems for exploring the ethical and epistemological problems of otherness while at the same time 'giving a form to oneself as a piece of difficult, refractory and suffering material' (a phrase he has quoted from Nietzsche) (*VP* 87).

One might begin by setting a poem by Hill alongside one by his contemporary, Seamus Heaney. Many (though not all) of Heaney's poems describe events in his own life, so that while we may in principle make the distinction between the bio-graphical author and the fictional persona created in the poem, the temptation to read that persona as in some sense Heaney himself, and to take the poet's life as guarantee of the authenticity of the poem, is almost irresistible. A Heaney poem such as 'The Tollund Man' is not about his own life but about ritual and political violence, making, as it does, an imaginative link between twentieth-century Ireland and prehistoric Den-mark, through the poet's reflections on a photograph of the mummified body of a victim of ritual murder. Yet it begins, 'Some day I will go to Aarhus' (where the body is kept in a museum) and ends 'I will feel lost,/ Unhappy and at home'.[3] The poet offers his own experience and his own subjectivity – where he has been or might go, and how he does or might feel – as frame and key to the meaning of the poem.

When asked by an interviewer about his 'avoidance' of confessional poetry, Hill replied: 'I don't take the confessional poetry quite seriously enough to think that I have to go to great lengths to try to avoid it – I just don't like it very much and get on with my own work' (*BF*). Yet Hill's poetry does clearly register the pressure, if not of 'confessional' poetry as such, at least of the lyric of individual subjectivity as I have outlined it above, and as practised by a highly accomplished contempor-ary such as Heaney. Hill's most discussed poem, 'September

9

Song', is, like 'The Tollund Man', about political violence; in this case the murder of a child by the Nazis. It is also about the risks of elegy: the risks of indulging in vicarious emotion and appropriating the suffering of others in order to create an aesthetic object (the poem). This poem does not begin with Hill's own experience (for example, imagining a trip to see a memorial to the dead child); it begins with the child's own experience – or at least, it attempts the highly problematic task of addressing that experience:

> Undesirable you may have been, untouchable
> you were not. Not forgotten
> or passed over at the proper time.
>
> As estimated, you died. Things marched,
> sufficient, to that end.
> Just so much Zyklon and leather, patented
> terror, so many routine cries.
>
> (KL 19)

While the tone here – intense, brooding, heavy with tragic irony – conveys a strong sense of Hill's ethical stance, the poet's subjectivity does not dominate the poem. Our attention is directed rather towards the language itself, in all its density, complexity, richness of meaning and history. The impression the reader gets is less that the poet has thoughts, feelings, and experiences and then puts them *into* words, than that the poetry is a form of discovery of shared meaning (especially historical and ethical) through a struggle *with* words. Ultimately, perhaps, this involves the discovery of a sense of selfhood; as Hill has commented 'one is ploughing down into one's own selfhood and into the deep strata of language at one and the same time. This takes effort and may be painful' (S 2). So in the opening lines of 'September Song' words such as 'undesirable', 'untouchable', and 'passed over' carry a heavy freight of loaded association: 'undesirable' compacts one of the most human of emotions, desire (including the poet's desire somehow to rescue the child) with the 'inhuman' bureaucratic horror of the racially 'undesirable' person; 'untouchable' suggests the physical vulnerability of the child as well as the idea of the social 'untouchable', and questions the validity of our being 'touched' by the suffering of the dead; 'passed over'

10

alludes with tragic irony to the Jewish festival of the Passover (commemorating the protection of the Jews from a slaughter of the first-born in Egypt, in Exodus). The poem's effect depends not only on word associations, but on tone, rhythm and syntax: the terseness and bitter calm of lines 4 and 5 (a four-word sentence and a six-word sentence, each with a sense of balance in their syntactical structure) enact the horror specific to the Nazi genocide: the fact that it was irrational hatred and violence organized through the methods of a modern, bureau-cratic state, with numbers and materials 'estimated', terror 'patented' (with an uneasy echo of 'patent leather'), and the cries of suffering 'routine'. Ambiguity and multiple meanings are crucial to this way of writing, and much critical analysis of the poem has focused on the ambiguous third stanza:

> (I have made
> an elegy for myself it
> is true)

(KL 19)

Here the line break between 'it' and 'is' encourages the reader to wonder whether the elegy is 'true' (appropriate) or whether it is true that the elegy is really 'for myself' – that elegies comfort the living but are of no use to the dead.

Whereas Heaney's poem places the poet's self at the beginning and end, enclosing the poem and its meanings, Hill's poem literally brackets his self in the middle third stanza. This bracketing indicates unease at the possibility of that self being taken as the guarantor of the poem's meaning and truth. The poem is about the way in which the dead child's experience is beyond recapture, or can be captured only by an aestheticization which risks the falsity suggested by Coleridge, whom Hill is in the habit of quoting on the subject of poetry and emotion: 'Poetry – excites us to artificial feelings – makes us callous to real ones'.[4] The final four lines emphasize the unbridgeable distance between the poet, in material comfort ('this is plenty' – with some of that word's Old Testament connotations of a savagely unpredictable divine dispensation)[5] and facing only a harmless September bonfire (amid the traditional elegiac associations of autumnal decay, here tinged with disgust in the word 'fattens'):

11

September fattens on vines. Roses
flake from the wall. The smoke
of harmless fires drifts to my eyes.

This is plenty. This is more than enough.

(KL 19)

The poem ends in a form of self-rebuke: even these terse words
are already 'plenty' and perhaps too much has been said. The
poet's self is both excluded from the poem and central to it, as
figured by the central but bracketed position of the 'I'. In a
sense the speaker's *failure* to encompass the child's experience
is the meaning of the poem, and as such stands for a failure in
our collective cultural memory and ethical imagination, just as
Heaney's conflicted ambivalence ('Unhappy and at home')
represents conflicted elements within Northern Irish culture.
Self and other are ethically implicated yet existentially estranged in 'September Song', and Hill obliquely signals this by
the poem's epigraph ('born 19.6.32. – deported 24.9.42.'), which
gives the dead child a birthday one day later than his own. The
basis of ethics is the ability to empathize imaginatively with
others, to 'identify' with their experience, including their
suffering. How does such identification relate to identity, and
when does it become appropriation (speaking for others,
projecting one's own needs or feelings onto them)? Is there an
opposition or a congruence between making a true elegy, and
making an elegy for oneself? That is to say, does imagining
oneself as the other acknowledge or efface the identity of the
other? Or, indeed, does it involve effacement of the self – has
Hill only succeeded in elegizing his own self-loss?

'September Song', first published in 1967, was collected in
Hill's second full-length volume of poetry, *King Log* (1968). His
first volume, *For the Unfallen* (1959), had centred around poems
on the violent history of modern Europe and poems of
religious faith, quest and doubt. Personal elements had been
notably lacking in *For the Unfallen*. Poems such as 'The Turtle
Dove', 'The Troublesome Reign' 'Asmodeus' and poem V of
'Metamorphoses', which evoke sexual and psychological conflicts through muscular syntax and dense, atmospheric imagery, surely drew on Hill's own experience at some level (and
the same would apply to a poem of inner religious conflict

such as 'The Bidden Guest'). However, any links to the poet's own life remain speculative and of limited relevance to a reading of the poems, which offer us verbal enactments of certain forms of experience, rather than the personality of the individual poet. Religious elements persist in *King Log*, but historical themes become more dominant, ranging further afield to early American history ('Locust Songs') and the English Wars of the Roses ('Funeral Music'). Elegiac commemorations of Hill's poetic forebears are a recurrent feature of his work, including 'Little Apocalypse' (on Hölderlin) in *For the Unfallen*, and, in *King Log*, 'Four Poems Regarding the Endurance of Poets' (elegies for four European poets, all victims of political oppression). These poems inevitably imply some reflection on the act of writing, its ethical, political and social meaning, but the dominant mood is that of paying tribute to the memory and suffering of these past masters. The moral risks attendant on the imagination and its creative activity are addressed in more general and more troubled terms in a number of poems, published between 1958 and 1967 and collected in *For the Unfallen* and *King Log*: 'Dr Faustus', 'A Pastoral', 'Orpheus and Eurydice', 'To the (Supposed) Patron', 'Annunciations', 'A Pre-Raphaelite Notebook', 'The Humanist', 'The Imaginative Life', 'History as Poetry' and 'Three Baroque Meditations'. In these poems the imaginative recall of the dead, the appreciation of high culture and the writing and reading of poetry are all represented in metaphors of distasteful, even cannibalistic consumption and voyeuristic indulgence. For example, in 'A Pastoral' and 'Orpheus and Eurydice' personified qualities – 'the Pities' or 'Love' – take part in allegorical journeys which serve ironically to impute voyeuristic motives or aesthetic detachment to such supposedly ethical attributes:

> Mobile, immaculate and austere,
> The Pities, their fingers in every wound,
> Assess the injured on the obscured frontier;
>
> ('A Pastoral', *FU* 56)

> Traversing the still-moist dead,
> The newly-stung,
>
> Love goes, carrying compassion
>   To the rawly-difficult;

> His countenance, his hands' motion,
> Serene even to a fault.
>
> ('Orpheus and Eurydice', *FU* 57)

This vein is given most sustained development in the first part of 'Annunciations', where the 'poetry-banquet' (as Hill terms it in his own commentary on the poem) is presented as 'conspicuous consumption' of a physical world of suffering which has been aestheticized and commodified for the complacent consumers.[6] Hill is satirizing the poetry scene of the early sixties here and the commodification of art in postmodern culture. However, he also directs considerable reflexive suspicion and even condemnation at his own work and especially at his own elegiac impulses. The reader may ask why Hill persisted in writing poetry, given these concerns, and it is a question he himself posed and tentatively answered, in an essay about the idea that writing is both a source of guilt and an act of atonement:

> Well, if one feels like this about it, why carry on? And why carry on so? And in public too! ... let us postulate yet another impure motive, remorse, and let us suggest that a man may continue to write and to publish in a vain and self-defeating effort to appease his own sense of empirical guilt. It is ludicrous, of course. (*LL* 7)

My own reading of Hill's poetry of this period is that it does indeed confront the possibility of silence, of ceasing to write, which would be one meaning of the last line of 'September Song'. This poem is both the culmination of this crisis in Hill's early poetry, and the beginning of its solution. It points the way to a solution precisely because it introduces the poet's 'I', even if hedged round with brackets and ambiguities. The crisis in Hill's early poetry springs out of the poet's powerful sense of two conflicting moral imperatives: to commemorate the dead (especially the victims of war and oppression) and to avoid speaking for the dead in such a way as to submerge their otherness in our own needs, fantasies and ideas. The self is clearly central to this problem, since it is a problem about who takes the responsibility for an utterance or text, and how their own experience, their own subject-position in the widest sense, relates to the life or lives commemorated. Hill's early, highly impersonal poetry, in which a condensed style effaces the self, tends towards radical ambiguity, in which the same words generate opposite meanings, and towards self-condemnation, in which the poem rebukes itself for exploiting its subject, and even rebukes itself for rebuking itself. Hill's images of poetry as repulsive consumption satirize a sentimental wallowing in pity, an emotional cannibalism of the sufferings of others. The problem is that, in seeming to criticize themselves for potential exploitation, the poems can also seem to congratulate themselves for their own tact or moral rigour; as Hill writes, in a strikingly physical image:

> For I am circumspect,
> Lifting the spicy lid of my tact
> To sniff at the myrrh.

> ('Three Baroque Meditations', sect. 2, *KL* 47)

As critics have pointed out, there is a risk here of infinite regress; awareness of tact can be an infringement of it, in the form of self-congratulation.[7]

By finding some place for the self in his poetry, Hill moves aside from the extremes of self-revoking paradox found in the second part of 'Annunciations', where, as Hill notes in his commentary, the phrase 'Our God scatters corruption' (sect. 2, *KL* 15) means two opposite things at once (our God destroys corruption; our God spreads corruption). In addressing self-hood more directly, Hill by no means abandons his resistance to the confessional or autobiographical, and nor does he abandon the process of discovering meaning through the struggle with the density and complexity of language. But in poems published between 1965 and 1971, notably 'The Song-book of Sebastian Arrurruz' and *Mercian Hymns*, he finds space for a more playful and humorous exploration of the paradoxes and complexities of self and other.

To achieve this exploration, Hill draws on the technique of personae used by modernist writers such as T. S. Eliot and Ezra Pound. In contrast to the autobiographical persona of a poet such as Heaney, the modernist poetic persona is charac-teristically an invented, historical or mythological character, whose relationship to the poet is marked by a mixture of identification and ironic distancing. Eliot in 'The Love Song of J. Alfred Prufrock' portrays an imaginary character with a mixture of sympathy and irony resembling Hill's treatment of Arrurruz. Pound in 'Hugh Selwyn Mauberley' uses an imaginary poet for the purposes of cultural critique, and for the ironic projection of aspects of his own cultural positioning. Pound's irony is such that there has been a long-running debate as to which parts of the sequence we should imagine as Mauberley's voice, and which as voicing Pound's own opinions.[8] The use of such character-personae wards off naively biographical readings, and enables subtle explorations of unity and multiplicity, stability and variety, within the self.

Hill's 'Sebastian Arrurruz' is an imaginary Spanish poet and we are given the dates of his life, 1868–1922, at the head of the sequence. Hill has said that his 'main inspiration for the idea was in the work of Antonio Machado' (a real Spanish poet, 1875–1939), who 'created an "apocryphal professor"' . . . and an imaginary poet-philosopher' (*VP* 95). Yet, given the importance of Pound and Eliot to Hill (evident, for example, from Hill's critical essays), the influence of Anglo-American modernism is also inescapable. Both Eliot's Prufrock and Hill's Arrurruz imagine what it would be like to have a different personality: Prufrock fantasizes a decisive and impressive self which he cannot attain, while Arrurruz, in the appropriately titled 'Postures', imagines 'that I am not myself/ But someone I might have been'. This suggests that the sequence may involve Hill imagining himself being someone else, which is neither self-expression nor confession, but is yet very different from the abnegation of self in the earlier poetry. Arrurruz is not Hill, but seems to have certain points in common with him, such as fastidiousness, a fondness for irony, an exacting approach to art and a strong sense of loss. Hill invites us to imagine Arrurruz as a real poet, as he regrets that 'the finer nuances' of Arrurruz's work 'have been lost in translation' (*VP* 95). Some critics have seen Hill as essentially a late modernist, and that case can certainly be made on the basis of the intensity and seriousness of his engagement with literary tradition, his dense, allusive style and his use of poetic sequences or 'pocket epics' to deploy history and myth as oblique critique of contemporary culture.[9] But, as R. K. Meiners acutely observes, 'when one has learned as deeply from modernism as Hill has, there can be no question of repeating it unknowingly'.[10] In

Pound's 'Hugh Selwyn Mauberley', a major focus of irony is the poet's troubled relationship with his own historical moment, the problem of how a poet 'out of key with his time' responds to what 'The age demanded'.[11] In echoing aspects of Pound's technique, some fifty years on, Hill (who often seems hostile to contemporary cultural tendencies) is adding a further historical irony, not perpetrating a naive repetition. This fact is signalled in Hill's comment that Arrurruz's date of death (1922) 'enabled him to die on the very threshold of modernity, without having had the advantage of reading *The Waste Land* or *Ulysses*' (*VP* 95) – these being two classic texts of high modernism in English. Whether such ironical redeployment of modernist strategies can appropriately be termed postmodernist is a question which cannot be explored fully here, given the complexity of debates over the meaning of the term 'postmodernism', though the relevance of the term to Hill's work will be considered further in relation to his treatment of history.[12] However, it can certainly be argued that Hill's playful manoeuvres around the borders of fictionality and textuality (such as his implication that he is translating fragments from a longer 'Songbook' in Spanish) partake of postmodernist blurring of the real and the fictional.

The ironical reflections on self and otherness in 'The Songbook', then, are not merely personal, but cultural and historical, as Hill ironizes his own relationship to literary tradition through a persona who is pre-modernist in biography, modernist in technique and postmodernist in his pseudo-textual (non)existence. In one sense, though, 'The Songbook of Sebastian Arrurruz' does represent a turn to the 'personal', in that it is primarily a sequence of love poems. Published in various sections before being put together into a sequence in *King Log* (1968), its publication dates cover the period 1965 to 1968, before and after the publication of 'September Song', and the continuities and differences between the two works reveal Hill's change of direction. The title of each poem suggests poetry conceived as song: a song of mourning and a love song (albeit primarily of lost love). In each the title is followed by a subtitle alluding to an individual and the dates of his or her life, but in 'September Song' the name is crucially absent. 'September Song' deals with

the themes which had preoccupied Hill since the mid-fifties:
the moral risks of poetry in its attempt to articulate suffering,
and to face the horrors of European history. But it also moves
on from the self-revoking, paradoxical rhetoric of his earlier
work by locating, however minimally, the poet as subject. 'The
Songbook' takes up relatively new themes, while its subtitle
names a fictional construct through whom the poet may
achieve a new lucidity, and sensuous immediacy. In places this
involves a conversational, largely monosyllabic style which is
powerful in its directness of feeling, as in the opening lines of
'Coplas', where Arrurruz addresses his estranged wife (or
possibly lover):

> 'One cannot lose what one has not possessed.'
> So much for that abrasive gem.
> I can lose what I want. I want you.
>
> (KL 54)

Elsewhere in the sequence a physicality, always present in
Hill's work but frequently tinged with disgust or violence,
finds a more lyrical expression, as in the ninth poem, 'A Song
from Armenia':

> A drinking-fountain pulses its head
> Two or three inches from the troughed stone.
> An old woman sucks there, gripping the rim.
>
> Why do I have to relive, even now,
> Your mouth, and your hand running over me
> Deft as a lizard, like a sinew of water?
>
> (KL 61)

Having stressed the ironical nature of 'The Songbook', it might
seem contradictory to write of its directness and simplicity, yet
the one proceeds from the other; as Gabriel Pearson has
suggested, 'the extreme irony of the mask . . . permits a release'
(GH 47). Yet 'The Songbook' is also an intensely literary,
self-conscious work, since Arrurruz's emotions of longing,
desire, melancholy, self-pity and resignation are interwoven
with, and figured by, his activities as poet, scholar and
archaeologist, and reveal a highly aestheticized, sometimes
pedantic but acutely sensitive sensibility, evident in the first
poem of the sequence:

Ten years without you. For so it happens.
Days make their steady progress, a routine
That is merciful and attracts nobody.

Already, like a disciplined scholar,
I piece fragments together, past conjecture
Establishing true sequences of pain;

(*KL* 53)

Here strong emotion emerges through understatement, suggesting pain now controlled and habitual, and an attitude of precision and stoicism. The 'steady progress' of the days is enacted by the steadiness of the opening lines, their clear syntax and short sentences or clauses. The 'true sequences of pain' include 'The Songbook' itself as a poetic sequence, as well as the chronological and emotional sequence of Arrurruz's life. Thus this phrase, like 'it/is true' in 'September Song', comments reflexively on the poem and there is a comparable (though less extreme) uncertainty: true to what? 'Past conjecture', a characteristically Hillian ambiguity, suggests conjecture about the past, conjectures made in the past, and also certainty (beyond conjecture). The last sense makes the phrase another reflexive assertion of truth (the sequence is true past conjecture). But there is also a suggestion that the fragmentation (of both feeling and language) may be past the ability of conjecture to reunite them, so that the sequence is true only as a fiction, and is false to the unity of experience which the fragments once composed. Fragmentation or multiplicity within the self is implicit here.

This subtle exploration of the intricacies of self informs the volume which followed *King Log*, and which forms a single sequence of prose poems, *Mercian Hymns*. But where 'The Songbook' establishes relations of self and other which combine identification with ironic distance, *Mercian Hymns* emphasizes ideas of mutuality and exchange. The reader is likely to be struck first by the formal and religious associations of the title and by the distinctive form (unusual in English) of the prose-poem. While Hill frequently uses such formal titles – naming his poems as 'songs', 'meditations', 'chorale preludes' or 'psalms' – his use of the prose poem is confined to *Mercian Hymns* and two sections of 'The Songbook'. Each of the thirty

19

'hymns' consists of between one and four 'versets of rhythmical prose', in Hill's own words (*VP* 93). The term 'verset' has liturgical associations: it can mean 'a little or short verse, especially one of the Bible' or 'one of a series of short sentences, usually taken from the Psalms and of a precatory [entreating or supplicating] nature, said or sung antiphonally in divine service' (*OED*). Hill's notes to the volume point to *Sweet's Anglo-Saxon Reader* as a source for the title, and mention 'the Latin prose-hymns or canticles of the early Christian Church'. Yet, in contrast to what the title, notes and Hill's formal terminology might lead one to expect, the sequence begins with comic historical anachronism, and soon introduces elements of personal memory and narrative; nor is it primarily a religious work. It may be that Hill's imagination requires a certain formality within which to indulge a certain informality, and that the prose-poem presented itself as an appropriately paradoxical form for such a combination.

The first hymn begins by announcing a series of attributes of the eighth-century King Offa of Mercia, associating him with the landscape and with constructions and artefacts, ancient and modern (including Offa's dyke, a rampart and ditch along the border between England and Wales):

> King of the perennial holly-groves, the riven sandstone:
>   overlord of the M5: architect of the historic
>   rampart and ditch, the citadel at Tamworth, the
>   summer hermitage in Holy Cross: guardian of the
>   Welsh bridge and the Iron bridge: contractor to the
>   desirable new estates:
>
> (MH, hymn I)[13]

This is a sort of hymn of praise, part serious and part ironic, addressed to Offa, who, in Hill's imaginative construction of him, figures as 'the presiding genius of the West Midlands'.[14] The co-presence in the sequence is that of Hill's child self, growing up in the West Midlands in the 1930s and 1940s. It should be added, though, that just as the figure of Offa is a mixture of historical king, mythic presence and imagined spirit of place, so the figure of the child is an imaginative and symbolic projection, not a piece of realistic autobiography, though elements of Hill's own childhood are used. The complex sense of identity evoked in the sequence is signalled in hymn II. Hymns I and II carry the title 'The Naming of Offa' (poem titles appear only in a list at the back of *Mercian Hymns* and on the Contents page of *Collected Poems*), and whereas hymn I historically disperses and reconstructs Offa, hymn II semantically and phonetically shuffles both 'Geoffrey' and 'Offa', in a series of plays on the versions, meanings, sounds and associations of the phonologically linked names: 'A specious gift' suggests a marketing 'special offer'/ Offa; 'curt graffito' alludes to the expression 'eff off' (Geoff off; eff Offa); 'A laugh; a cough' offers two sound equivalents for Geoff or Offa, and so on.

Mercian Hymns meditates on history, landscape, political power, violence, aesthetics, memory and time by interweaving the acts of a king with the games of a child, so that, for example, a little boy's sense of loss and fantasies of power and consolation become intermeshed with the paranoia and child-ishness of a ruler:

> Ceolred was his friend and remained so, even after
>   the day of the lost fighter: a biplane, already
>   obsolete and irreplaceable
>   . . .
> After school he lured Ceolred, who was sniggering
>   with fright, down to the old quarries, and flayed
>   him.
>
> (MH, hymn VII)

> Threatened by phone-calls at midnight, venomous
>   letters, forewarned I have thwarted their
>   imminent devices.
>
> (MH, hymn VIII)

Despite Hill's insistence that the poem is not 'confessional', one aspect of *Mercian Hymns* is analogous to the *Künstlerroman* (the story of the development of the author's mind). In its depiction of the intimate relationship between the child's growing sensibility and the landscape, it recalls Wordsworth's *Prelude*. As with Wordsworth, though, the personal material is de-ployed in the service of philosophical and psychological reflections on developmental and creative processes. *Mercian Hymns* is pervaded by images and descriptions which work reflexively as metaphors for the processes of writing poetry (and especially *this* poetry), and for the processes upon which that creative act depends, such as those of memory, research, discovering and uncovering, observation and recording, inter-textual exchange and allusion: 'Their spades grafted through the variably-resistant soil'; 'I have raked up a golden and stinking blaze' (*MH*, hymn XII); 'Trim the lamp; polish the lens; draw, one by one, rare coins to the light' (*MH*, hymn XIII); 'He had a care for natural minutiae. What his gaze touched was his tenderness' (*MH*, hymn XIV); 'this master-mason as I envisage him, intent to pester upon tympanum and chancel-arch his moody testament' (*MH*, hymn XXIV). These allusions to aspects of Mercian life in the eighth and twentieth centuries also serve as images for the writing of poetry. The imagining of the past in chthonic or archaeological terms has affinities here with the work of Heaney who, like Hill, uses images of the ground and the remains that it holds, together with ideas of language as a repository, to explore the collective cultural past and represent the accumulations of personal memory and unconscious.[15] In *Mercian Hymns* Hill discovered a way of writing about his own childhood without using the confessional mode. Mutuality is crucial to this achievement: Offa's reign and Hill's childhood co-exist, neither being subordinated as metaphor for the other. Both Hill and Offa have a voice in the sequence, but neither is its sole origin; rather they share in a linguistic continuum. Thus the first hymn concludes with Offa's comment on his own naming: ' "I liked that," said Offa, "sing it again." '. Like the poet, Offa is listening to a song about himself, speaking in the hymn which also speaks of him.

In the penultimate hymn the poet (like Heaney in 'Digging') writes of his complex relationship to his family roots (as well as to Offa):[16]

> 'Not strangeness, but strange likeness. Obstinate,
>   outclassed forefathers, I too concede. I am
>   your staggeringly-gifted child.'

(MH, hymn XXIX)

The 'strange likeness' acknowledged is both with family and ancestors ('outclassed' in literary and social terms, yet in some degree the source of that strange temperament) and with Offa.

In both respects this recognition of 'strange likeness' represents a degree of reconciliation, after the sense of immitigable loss in 'September Song' and the ironic self-consciousness of 'The Songbook'. A clue to the source of this reconciliation may be found in the phrase from hymn VI: 'I . . . gave myself to unattainable toys'. The sense of the lost and unattainable, of the 'lost kingdom of innocence and original justice' to which Hill has alluded in interview, is a key element of his work and his sensibility.[17] *Mercian Hymns* is not Hill's *Paradise Regained*: his lost kingdom is not the sort that can be regained through art, though art can 'bear witness' to it. But it is a recognition of what is *not* lost, an exploration of both continuities and discontinuities. The phrase 'gave myself' carries an unusual weight here, meaning not just childish absorption but a giving up of the self to that which cannot be obtained. The mutuality between the boy and Offa represents a new, paradoxical form of impersonality, in which a giving over of the self, to the other, to the unattainable, to the past, makes possible a greater sense of mutuality and thus a certain retrieving of the self. It is perhaps this which enables a unique moment in Hill's oeuvre when, in hymn XXV, he speaks as himself, deliberately, explicitly and without irony or paradox (though with a formal self-consciousness):

> Brooding on the eightieth letter of *Fors Clavigera*,
> I speak this in memory of my grandmother,
> whose childhood and prime womanhood were
> spent in the nailer's darg.

The first line alludes to John Ruskin's *Fors Clavigera: Letters to the Workmen and Labourers of Great Britain* (1871–84), a critique of social injustice and the exploitation of labourers under capitalism, and more specifically to a letter of 16 July 1877 in which Ruskin describes visiting a house near Bewdley, Worcestershire, where he observes two women labouring at the cottage industry of nail making, and notes the hard conditions of their labour, their long 'darg' ('a day's work, the task of a day') and poor wages.[18] Hill describes his personal connection to this industry in his interview with John Haffenden:

> On my mother's side I'm descended from artisans in the tradi-
> tional cottage-industry of nail-making. As a child and young

23

woman my grandmother was a nailer, making hand-made nails. I felt very close to her; I realize retrospectively how close the attachment was. During my childhood my mother was seriously ill on two occasions, and I lived with my grandmother at those times, in her tiny cottage at the end of a row. It had a small garden with an ancient damson tree and an old shed which still contained my dead grandfather's carpenter's tools. (*VP* 76)

The second and third versets of the hymn evoke the setting of his grandmother's labour with a lyrical beauty while emphasizing its harshness and the damage to her health. These lines also acknowledge the inaccessibility of dead lives to our designs or consolations, while suggesting the inviolable nature of the poet's sensory memory of the scene, and conveying its personal and ethical meaning:

> The nailshop stood back of the cottage, by the fold.
> It reeked stale mineral sweat. Sparks had furred
> its low roof. In dawn-light the troughed water
> floated a damson-bloom of dust –
>
> not to be shaken by posthumous clamour. It is one
> thing to celebrate the 'quick forge', another to
> cradle a face hare-lipped by the searing wire.[19]

(MH, hymn XXV)

The hymn ends with an exact repetition of the first verset, forming a sort of chorus, and emphasizing Hill's act of commemoration. The retrospective realization of closeness is important to *Mercian Hymns* as a whole, with its insistence that the past (personal and historical) cannot be reclaimed but, in its 'strange likeness', must not be forgotten. The sequence by no means forgets the horrors of histories which so much preoccupied Hill's earlier work. Indeed hymn XVIII is one of his most disturbing treatments of violence and voyeurism, and the sequence, in Hill's words, uses 'the murderous brutality of Offa as a political animal' as 'an objective correlative for the ambiguities of English history in general', even while it pays tribute to his achievements (*VP* 94). *Mercian Hymns* recognizes the impulses of violence, paranoia and power-seeking within the self, expressed through both kingly violence and boyhood games. This dark vein, though, is combined with (and partially offset by) the ideas of giving, exchange and reciprocity which echo through the sequence from the mock-grandiloquence of hymn X ('he exchanged gifts with the Muse of History') to the ambivalent image of a sword in hymn XVI ('The Frankish gift, two-edged, regaled with slaughter ... And other miracles, other exchanges') and the gratitude and humorous hubris of hymn XXIX ('I am your staggeringly-gifted child'). The two imaginative personalities of the sequence, the poet and Offa, do not achieve any transcendent, timeless unity, but they might be seen as exchanging imaginative possessions, and in this way *Mercian Hymns* nevertheless achieves a more recipro-cal vision of the relation of self and other.

As already suggested, Hill's poetry frequently engages in some form of dialogue or exchange with other poets. One form which this takes is his writing of translations, or more often versions, of poetry in other languages. *Tenebrae*, as Hill's notes inform us, includes several poems which imitate, freely trans-late, or take as a starting point, poems in Spanish or German. Of these, 'Two Chorale-Preludes' immediately signals by its subtitle ('on melodies by Paul Celan') both a strong debt to the German poet named, and a relationship between Hill's poems and Celan's originals which is one of musical reworking rather than translation. Hill's notes (*CP* 204) identify the main source poems from Celan's *Die Niemandsrose* (1963) – 'Eis, Eden' ('Ice, Eden') and 'Kermorvan' – adding 'I have combined a few phrases of free translation with phrases of my own invention'. This rather dry, scrupulously accurate comment does not convey the extent to which Hill's poems inhabit and rework the sensibility expressed in Celan's enigmatic yet compelling language of metaphor and symbol. Such a free reworking across two languages itself represents a negotiation of self and otherness, a voicing of self through the voice of another poet, foregrounding what is true of all language, that it exists before, after and outside the consciousness of its users, giving a form to their identity or selfhood even as their speech is itself given form by that self. The self both finds itself and loses itself in language. For Celan, a (German-speaking) Romanian poet who survived a labour camp during World War II, the German language, intimately his own yet associated with the Nazi regime which murdered his parents along with millions of others, was especially precious yet problematic. He said that language was the only thing that remained intact for him after the war.[20] By terming his poems 'Chorale-Preludes' Hill evokes a musical form which includes both counterpoint between original melody (hymn tunes) and accompaniment, and allusion to an absent text. Thus in Bach's chorale preludes from the *Orgel-Büchlein* (composed 1715–16):

> the chorale is normally presented as a continuous melody . . . to a contrapuntal accompaniment in the lower parts whose constant and unified motivic material, although almost always unrelated to the melodic substance of the chorale, is suggested by the emotional content or theological symbolism of the text. In effect, the chorale text, silent but implied by the traditional melody, is presented simultaneously with its exegesis by the counter-voices.[21]

Hill reminds us of the implicit presence of the chorale or hymn text, by giving his two poems the titles of well-known Latin hymns: 'Ave Regina Coelorum' (or, 'Salve Regina': 'Hail, Queen of Heaven') and 'Te Lucis Ante Terminum' ('Thee before the close of day'). The silent presence of the absent (unsung) text in a chorale prelude has a special appropriateness to Celan's theme of the home (literal and metaphorical) which is absolutely lost and yet integral to the self (Celan described his poems as 'a sort of homecoming').[22] Hill's first poem begins 'There is a land called Lost/ at peace inside our heads', echoing the opening line of Celan's 'Ice, Eden', 'Es ist ein Land Verloren' ('There is a country Lost'). His second poem paradoxically evokes 'midsummer closeness my far home,/ fresh traces of lost origin', echoing Celan's 'Kermorvan', 'mit euch Nahen geh ich ins Ferne, –/ Wir gehen dir, Heimat, ins Garn' ('with you near ones I make for afar, –/ to our homeland, snared, we return').[23] In title, form, theme and imagery, the 'Two Chorale-Preludes' represent forms of transformation of otherness within language, music and the self. The second stanza of Hill's first poem condenses some of the paradoxes of the self: its estrangement and self-discovery in language; the split between the self which reflects and the self which is reflected upon, involved in any reflection of/ on the self:

> Moods of the verb 'to stare',
> split selfhoods, conjugate

ice-facets from the air,
the light glazing the light.

(T 35)

The 'moods' of an English verb are declarative, interrogative and imperative, while to 'conjugate' a verb is to list its inflexions – its various endings according to person and number. Bearing in mind that the verb gloss can mean 'to comment upon, explain, interpret', but also 'to render bright and glossy; to glaze' (OED), we might say that, through these grammatical metaphors, Hill glosses Celan's dispersal of the sense of self across mutually perceiving persons:

Es sieht, es sieht, wir sehen,
ich sehe dich, du siehst.

It sees, it sees, we see,
I see you, you see me.[24]

By exploring questions of selfhood, memory, identity and language via a textual and imaginative engagement with another writer, Hill achieves a form of lyric which is neither self-expression in the conventional sense, nor wholly impersonal.

This achievement is continued in more extended form in his 1983 book-length poem, *The Mystery of the Charity of Charles Péguy*, a sequence of 100 quatrains (the lines being loose iambic pentameters), variously rhymed abba, aabb or abab (with many half-rhymes) and arranged into ten sections of varying lengths. Focusing on the life, death and historical context of the French poet Charles Péguy (born 1873, killed during the Battle of the Marne, 1914), the sequence is a meditation on matters such as war, moral responsibility, memory and history, nostalgia and nationalism, but has inevitably provoked speculation as to the degree of Hill's identification with his subject. John Kerrigan argues that 'almost everything in the author's note makes you think of Geoffrey Hill on Hill as well as on [Péguy] ... Hill warily descries his own in another's features'.[25] However, the positive view of Péguy offered in the author's note (in fact a short essay on Péguy's life, appended to the poem) needs to be distinguished from the more ambivalent stance of the poem. (Hill's poetry does tend to be more dialogic and less defensive than his prose.) Grevel Lindop argues that we find in the poem the childhood landscape of *Mercian Hymns* superimposed on the Beauce (Péguy's home terrain in France), as though 'to suggest that we can only understand the meaning of other people's myths by gathering to them some of the emotion that interpenetrates our own'.[26] Nevertheless, a comparison of *The Mystery* with *Mercian Hymns* suggests crucial differences between Hill and Péguy. *Mercian Hymns* is partly about a child growing up in wartime, not old enough to be involved, but loving 'the battle-anthems and the gregarious news' (*MH*, hymn XXII). Péguy's childhood, on the other hand, is presented in Hill's poem as a preparation for, even a prophecy of, his death in battle:

> On the hard-won
> high places the old soldiers of old France
> crowd like good children wrapped in obedience
>
> and sleep, and ready to be taken home.
> Whatever that vision, it is not a child's;
> it is what a child's vision can become.
>
> (*M* 2.3–2.4)[27]

Here Péguy's patriotic vision is presented as vitiated by a sentimentality which is not that of a child, but which, Hill speculates, may have grown out of the fantasies and intense attachments of childhood, viewed retrospectively and endowed with political significance. This idea is developed in section 5 of the poem, where the child's toy soldiers are made to presage the casualties of real war: 'winds drumming the fame/ of the tin legions lost in haystack and stream' (*M* 5.10). Hill is a non-combatant survivor of a World War, whereas Péguy was a casualty of one. The importance of this to Hill's imagination, preoccupied as it is with the moral issues surrounding violent death, and its commemoration in art, cannot easily be overestimated. Furthermore, Hill ironizes his own childhood fantasies in *Mercian Hymns*, using Offa to suggest their links to some of the sources of real violence. Thus the figure of the child is mediated by an adult self who sees the dangers of 'what a child's vision can become'. But in *The Mystery*, Hill implicitly criticizes the adult Péguy for failing to realize fully this danger. Interpretations of the poem as oblique autobiography therefore tend to underrate crucial differences in experience and attitude between Hill and his subject. What Hill may do is to reflect his own guilt off Péguy's very different guilt: the guilt of the survivor about the inadequacy of his words, against the guilt of the dead polemicist, whose words may have been all too effective: 'Did Péguy kill Jaurès? Did he incite/ the assassin?' (*M* 1.4), asks the poem, alluding to the murder of the French socialist deputy Jean Jaurès, by 'a young madman' ('Charles Péguy', *M* 30) who may have been influenced by Péguy's criticisms of Jaurès.

Jeffrey Wainwright draws attention to the contiguity of words and things in the last line of the poem ('in memory of those things these words were born'), and sees *The Mystery* as a poem about words and what can be done with them:

> Hill's whole poem travels over these two possibilities: circumstances in which the self-sufficiency, the given facts of the world, events themselves, are moved by words, and circumstances – poetry itself may well be one – where words seem without real object and yet are 'moving'. (*GH* 101)

Of the two possibilities Wainwright describes, one is the source of Péguy's possible guilt, in that his words may have contributed to violent events, while the other is the source of Hill's sense of guilt, in that his words may excite feelings while remaining detached from reality. Thus Péguy offers Hill a mirror image of his own sense of guilt. A poet who did not take part in war (being only a child), who survived, who fears that his words may excite artificial feelings, writes about a poet who did take part, who died, whose words may have excited violent actions. The translinguistic word-games of *The Mystery*, as when the poem describes itself in French and English terms ('*éloge* and elegy', *M* 10.11 – *éloge* being French for eulogy), suggest an identification and difference between Hill and Péguy, the English and the French poets. While a degree of affinity between Hill and Péguy is important, it is the antithetical nature of Péguy's fate as a poet that needs to be emphasized.

Although *Canaan* (1996) contained both individual lyrics, and a number of short- to medium-length sequences, the non-narrative book-length poetic sequence has since become established as Hill's most important form, as *The Triumph of Love* (1998) and *Speech! Speech!* (2000) have continued, in very different ways, the precedent earlier established by *Mercian Hymns* and *The Mystery of the Charity of Charles Péguy*. (*Orchards of Syon* (2002) continues this trend, being a sequence of seventy-two sections, each of twenty-four lines.) Although various in their subject matter, structure and technique, each of these volumes constitutes a single, multi-part poem which, while including fragments of narrative and description, is essentially neither narrative (in the sense of telling a story) nor descriptive. While the ordering principle of *Mercian Hymns* was mutual exchange between modern child and ancient king, and *The Mystery* revolved around reflections on the life and times of Péguy, *The Triumph of Love* and *Speech! Speech!* take the form of a dialogue or cacophony of multiple voices. The voice of Hill's own persona is a persistent linking thread, but is constantly interrupted, undercut and quarrelled with, from within and without, by other voices and other discourses. These works bring Hill somewhat closer to those forms of postmodernist or avant-garde poetry which displace subjectivity into discursive multiplicity, partly in response to the deconstruction of subjectivity in postmodern literary and cultural theory. Yet, characteristically, Hill's trajectory remains unique.

While *Speech! Speech!* in particular registers the presence of a media- and discourse-saturated postmodern culture which has seemed to many cultural theorists to make the idea of the authentic self obsolete or untenable, Hill's recent volumes nevertheless defiantly reassert the importance of selfhood. As W. S. Milne notes:

> The word 'self' turns up time and time again in both volumes, usually in compounds, to emphasise the solipsism of experience: 'self-love'; 'self-extinction'; 'self-hatred'; 'self grafted to unself' (a fine definition of grief); 'self-pleasured'; 'self-disgust'; and, finally, humorously, 'self, the lost cause to end all/ lost causes'.[28]

In *The Triumph of Love* (1998) we see the fruition of Hill's realization, dating back to 'September Song', that a poetry which attempts to do justice to the dead victims of history must find a space for the poet's selfhood, while avoiding commodified, trivialized or sentimentalized forms of 'person-ality'. This long sequence of 150 sections (the same number as the Psalms in the Old Testament), ranging in length from one line to fifty-seven lines, is both Hill's most personal poem since *Mercian Hymns* and a poem which returns to one of the early preoccupations of his poetry – the many victims of the wars and atrocities of the twentieth century. The self-knowledge and self-criticism which Hill espoused in the *Paris Review* interview are seen as dependent upon a certain gratitude to previous generations, when understanding is defined as 'actuated self-knowledge, a daily acknowledgement/ of what is owed the dead' (*TL*, sect. CXIX).[29] For Hill knowledge of self is not a matter of pure introspection nor of untrammelled self-expression, but depends upon an ethical appreciation of our personal and collective obligations to others. The interdependence of self and other is explored in a dense and difficult passage of what is in effect philosophical argument:

> If I were to grasp once, in emulation,
> work of the absolute, origin-creating mind,
> its *opus est*, conclusive
> otherness, the veil
> of certitude discovered as itself
> that which is to be revealed,
> I should hold for my own, my self-giving,
> my retort upon Emerson's 'alienated majesty',
> the *De Causa Dei* of Thomas Bradwardine.

(*TL*, sect. VIII)

Here 'self-giving' (another 'self' compound to add to Milne's list) echoes the theme of giving in *Mercian Hymns* and stands in opposition to 'Self-reliance', which is the title of an essay by the American nineteenth-century philosopher and poet Ralph Waldo Emerson. This essay includes the passage alluded to in the next line ('Emerson's "alienated majesty" '):

> To believe your own thought, to believe that what is true for you in your private heart is true for all men, – that is genius ... our first thought is rendered back to us by the trumpets of the Last Judgment ... In every work of genius we recognize our own rejected thoughts; they come back to us with a certain alienated majesty.[30]

Hill's 'retort' to this assertion of the power of the individual mind is to allude to the fourteenth-century English theologian Thomas Bradwardine, whose *De Causa Dei* attacked the Pelagian heresy, the belief that 'the human will is of itself capable of good without the assistance of divine grace' (*OED*); Bradwardine insisted on 'the necessity of grace and the "irresistible" efficacy of the Divine Will, which is the cause of all action'.[31] So Hill seems to be insisting here on the need for a 'conclusive otherness' (whether one takes this in a theological sense, as God, or in a more psychological sense, as the Other) – an otherness which is not merely our own thought reflected back at us. Michael Edwards points out that the phrase 'in emulation' may allude to T. S. Eliot's 'East Coker': 'And what there is to conquer . . . has already been discovered/ Once or twice, or several times, by men whom one cannot hope/ To emulate'.[32] Eliot's lines represent an inversion of Emerson's idea: not a recognition that absolute truth merely echoes our own thoughts, but a recognition that our own thoughts are merely pale echoes of what has already been 'discovered'. The 'absolute, origin-creating mind' in Hill's poem might be the artist or God, and suggests perhaps the way in which the artist emulates God in the act of creation; *'opus est'* echoes a phrase from Virgil's *Aeneid* ('Hoc opus, hic labor est'), where it refers to the difficulty of a labour (in the original, that of returning from the underworld).[33] Hill's sense of the inherently paradoxical nature of the relations between selfhood and otherness is reflected in the statement here that 'my self-giving' (at once a defining of self and a giving out, or even giving up, of self) finds its point of certitude (the subjective conviction of the mind, as opposed to the objective 'certainty' of a proposition (*OED*)) precisely in a recognition of its own dependence on the other. The term 'certitude' has often been used in the context of religious faith, which requires a certain giving, or giving up, of the individual rational judgement in order to achieve a certitude which is held to be of the self but beyond it, requiring grace. Hence the paradoxical idea that what is discovered when 'the veil/ of certitude' (the mind's conviction of its own rightness, as implied by Emerson's doctrine) is withdrawn, is precisely that certitude, but transformed as emulation: a certitude in relation to the other rather than an imposition of the self on the world. Characteristically, Hill uses theology as a way of thinking about philosophical, psychological and even political issues. The appealing confidence of Emerson's doctrine acquires a potentially more sinister tinge when one reflects that 'to believe that what is true for you in your private heart is true for all men', while it might indicate an aspiration to universal sympathy, could also betray the delusions of omniscience and omnipotence underlying political tyranny and cultural imperialism. In a comparable point, Hill commented in 1981 that the heresy of Averroism (belief in the existence of a single Intellect or soul for the whole of humanity) at first seemed comforting, but later came to seem 'the archetype of the totalitarian state' (*VP* 98).

As will be obvious from this brief and far from exhaustive attempt to read nine lines, the density of allusion and subtlety of thought in *The Triumph of Love* means that many sections require detailed explication, yet the poem also includes powerful and immediate metaphors and images (see, for example, sect. LXXV), the lucid rhetoric of moral indignation (for example, sect. LXXVII), and moments of deliberately bathetic and crude humour (for example, sect. CV). Some sections of the poem return to the material of *Mercian Hymns*: the poet's childhood self ('I gather I was a real swine', *TL*, sect. LXXXII) and memories ('a washed-out day at Stourport or the Lickey,/ improvised rainhats mulch for papier-mâché', *TL*, sect. LIII), the West Midlands region where he grew up ('Sun-blazed, over Romsley, a livid rain-scarp', *TL*, sect. I), as well as the wartime period. But in place of the uneasy but creative exchange with the semi-mythical Offa, we have a heated antagonism with the voices of contemporary critics and enemies, introducing a relatively new note of informality into Hill's work. Hill imagines what others might say about him – 'Rancorous, narcissistic old sod – what/ makes him go on?' (*TL*, sect. XXXIX) and responds in kind: 'And yes – bugger you, MacSikker et al., – I do/ mourn and resent your desolation of learning' (*TL*, sect. CXIX). The voices Hill gives to his enemies and detractors are arguably too crude, so that the device can seem a pre-emptive form of self-assertion. But he does not only excoriate his enemies as ignorant and vulgar; he is also harshly self-critical. The crucial halfway poem (*TL*, sect. LXXV) admits that 'now I am half-way/ and lost – need I say – in this maze of my own/ devising'. This is modest in one sense, but not in another, since it echoes Dante's *Divine Comedy* and T. S. Eliot's *Four Quartets*.[34] However, Hill's persona is interrupted in his own acknowledgement of faults ('I am too much moved by hate') by the voice of the Virgin, who lists other faults: 'add greed, self-pity, sick/ scrupulosity, frequent fetal regression, *and/* a twisted libido?'

Hill's next volume, *Speech! Speech!* ironizes, even in its title, the idea of poetry as authentic personal speech, a result of 'finding your voice'. Instead of the romantic dream of pure, 'authentic' speech, the sequence conveys the sense of poetry, responsive to the multiple discourses of modern and contemporary culture (film, comedy, popular music, philosophy, medicine, sport) but also labouring under the pressure of the expectations of a trivialized public sphere. That the demands of an admiring crowd might presage the corruption of poetry rather than its triumph is signalled clearly enough by the cover-picture of a large, applauding crowd, caricatured at the front, fading rapidly into an amorphous mass towards the back. Although this cover, and the title, might suggest a continuation of the embattled stance of Hill's volume of essays, *The Enemy's Country* (the title of which expresses Hill's sense of the 'vast apparatus of Opinion' as a hostile environment for the poet, *EC* pp. xi–xii), *Speech! Speech!* engages with the contemporary world with humour and playfulness, interweaving many different discourses, voices and texts.

If some critics have suspected Hill of vatic portentousness, he shows himself ready in *Speech! Speech!* to acknowledge and deflect such a risk through parody and self-parody:

> Erudition. Pain. Light. Imagine it great
> unavoidable work; although: heroic
> verse a non-starter, says PEOPLE. Some believe
> we over-employ our gifts.

$$(SS\ 1)^{35}$$

Although *The Triumph of Love* and *Speech! Speech!* in many ways represent a radical departure for Hill in style and technique, the latter volume also sums up and revisits many of the preoccupations and themes of his poetry. The first three words above (which are the opening words of the poem) are as compact and telling a summary of that poetry as one could wish for: the erudition, or learning always present in Hill's allusions, epigraphs, quotations and in the intellectual level of his work; the pain which so often pervades it, as it records the suffering of so many throughout history while itself always seeming troubled or pained by its own problematic status; the light which breaks through in those moments of incandescent lyrical beauty which offer some consolation for the pain. Having offered this masterly, yet ironically brisk summation, the poem immediately turns on itself to state and mock the intellectual and moral ambition which must drive such creation, an ambition involving the need to believe that poetry can be both 'great' and necessary ('unavoidable'). 'Imagine it' hovers between affirming the power of the imagination and the colloquial sense of the word implying delusion (he imagines he is doing great work, the deluded fool!). Then, introducing the key note of the volume, we hear the voice of the ironically capitalized 'PEOPLE', which I would take to embrace both actual individual reactions and the constructed, manipulative, ideologically deployed 'voice of the people' which emerges through the contemporary media. While some people (and perhaps the 'PEOPLE') are suspicious of heroic verse, some critics may not have welcomed Hill's new productiveness at the century's end (three volumes of poetry published in four years and another soon to follow): 'Some believe we overemploy our gifts' remarks Hill's persona, humorously adopting the royal 'we' in parody of his own alleged tendency to take himself too seriously.[36]

The opening section continues by evoking, in satirical tone, aspects of the contemporary public sphere. First 'identical/ street parties' seems to allude to the millennium celebrations – a later section refers scathingly to the 'millennial/ doommood' and its lack of relevance to real spiritual understanding (*SS* 97). Then 'confusion, rapid exposure' (with the media sense of 'exposure' seeming most relevant) introduces the theme of chaotic and degraded forms of public life in an 'Age of mass consent' (*SS* 22), with a particular focus on the iniquities of the media:

These I imagine are the humble homes
the egalitarian anti-élitist SUN
condescends to daily.

(*SS* 37)

Section 1 then proposes, ironically, the poet's response: 'practise self-emulation'. The word 'emulation', used seriously in
The Triumph of Love as part of a theological argument and
echoing T. S. Eliot (see above), recurs here in a paradoxical
compound ('self-emulation') which undermines the modesty
implicit in the word. To echo one's own earlier work (as Hill
does so often in *Speech! Speech!*) is to practise a form of
self-emulation, but the phrase also suggests the risks of
solipsism and cultural isolation faced by the poet in a culture
with which he feels at odds; a culture which tends to reduce
poetry to background muzak: 'music for crossed/ hands; for
two fingers; music/ for taxiing to take off; for cremation.' The
concluding lines of section 1 restate further concerns of Hill's
work: his critique of a destructive lack of knowledge of, and
respect for, the past ('Archaic means | files pillaged and eras-
ed/ in one generation'); the problems of temporal and ethical
distance in relation to the past and to the dead ('Judge the
distance'); innocence and complicity, especially in relation to
suffering as a public spectacle ('Innocent bystanders on stand-
by. Painful/ scenes mar final auto-da-fé').[37]

Section 3 shows again the complementarity of self and other
in Hill's poetic discourse. The opening lines are autobiographical in subject matter, alluding to the successful treatment of
depression which Hill describes in his *Paris Review* interview:

How is it tuned, how can it be un-
tuned, with lithium, this harp of nerves? Fare well
my daimon,

The breaking of 'untuned' across the lines signals a metaphorical use of the rhythms of poetry for the emotional rhythms of
the self, while 'Fare well/ my daimon' suggests a connection
between his former depression and certain aspects of Hill's
poetic creativity; a daimon suggests an other (an attendant
spirit, demon or 'genius') which haunts but also inspires. The
section continues in a pastiche of the style of Gerard Manley
Hopkins (hyphenated neologistic compounds, the key Hop-

kins word 'stress', the imagery of flight, whether of angel or bird):

> inconstant
> measures, mood- and mind-stress, heart's rhythm
> suspensive; earth-stalled | the wings of suspension.

The constant 'measures' (lines) of Hill's highly wrought earlier poetry (now succeeded by 'the uneloquent [as] a form of eloquence', *PR* 289), may have sprung in part out of the 'inconstant measures' (changing self-estimation, or shifting emotional rhythms) of his 'chronic depression . . . accompanied by various exhausting obsessive-compulsive phobias' (*PR* 288). The phrase 'heart's rhythm/ suspensive' may allude to heart problems which Hill experienced shortly before his move to America, while the next phrase seems to evoke a loss of confidence or loss of inspiration: 'earth-stalled | the wings of suspension'.

Here then, as so often, Hill defines the self, or his self, through others, but with a greater element of biographical frankness than previously. Other poets whom he admires have especially played this role in his work. The self is found, or shaped, in language, yet language is something shared, and public, as well as intimate and private. Hence both the pleasures of reciprocity (as Hill explores aspects of his own experience through elements of the style of Hopkins) and the fear of language's corruption and misappropriation, to which section 3 turns next:

> To persist without sureties | take
> any accommodation. What if Scattergood
> Commodity took all?

'Scattergood Commodity' sounds like a modern addition to the allegorical figures of Bunyan's *Pilgrim's Progress*, representing the profligate dispersal of commodified culture under late capitalism, while 'accommodation' carries its older sense of compromise, here with pejorative implication. The response is a shift to ironic retreat:

> Very well | you
> shall have on demand, by return, *presto*,
> my contractual retraction.

>   Laser it off the barcode or simply
>   cut here –

Hill's technique here, as in many sections of *Speech! Speech!*, is to use the language of commerce, business and the law to comment on the fate of poetry and the dilemmas of the poet; in part using that language in punning or metaphorical senses, but also using it to stress the involvement of poetry in the realms of what he terms, in *The Enemy's Country*, 'negotium'.[38] This technique goes back a long way in his poetry and prose, as in the use of words like 'consultants' in 'A Pastoral' (*FU*) and 'speculate' in 'To the (Supposed) Patron' (*FU*), or in the title and theme of 'Our Word is Our Bond' (which applies the motto of the London Stock Exchange to matters of poetic responsibility) (*LL* 138–59). What is new in *Speech! Speech!*, however, is the extensive use of colloquialism ('by return, *presto*') and the language of contemporary technology ('Laser it off the bar-code'). The poems mentioned above from *For the Unfallen* tended to occupy a mythic realm, even if contemporary resonances are implicit. *Speech! Speech!*, though its 120 sections recall (or so the cover tells us) the 120 days of Sodom of the Marquis de Sade (mentioned also in section 96), is unequivocally of the turn of the twenty-first century, though it also looks back over the twentieth, with references to: 'satellite failure' (*SS*, sect. 22), the Internet (*SS*, sect. 26) and 'WORKERS' PLAYTIME' on 'Aunty Beeb' (*SS*, sect. 17).[39] The reflexive element so frequently present in Hill's poetry (the way in which it discusses its own status, nature, procedures and dilemmas) is very much to the fore in *Speech! Speech!* As in *The Triumph of Love*, Hill allows his own personality and his own public persona to enter into the poem's field of vision, but this personal element is mediated and inflected by what Hill himself terms 'autobiographical comedy, or even clownishness' (*PR* 284). In section 6 of *Speech! Speech!* he seems to return to the subject of those poetic gifts which some may think he over-employs:

>   They invested – were invested – in proprieties,
>   where cost can outweigh reward. Decency, duty,
>   fell through the floorboards (*applause*). I cannot
>   do more now than gape or grin
>   haplessly.

Many words and phrases in *Speech! Speech!* revisit earlier images from Hill's poetry. Here 'fell through the floorboards' may recall the toy dropped through the floorboards in *Mercian Hymns*, hymn VII. More importantly, 'invested' is a significant echo of the same volume: 'I was invested in mother-earth, the crypt of roots and endings. Child's-play.' (*MH*, hymn IV). This earlier use of the word 'investment' implies both that the child Hill was a literary 'investment' on the part of his parents or country, and that his childhood experiences served to invest him with the sensibility of a poet (in the sense of invest defined as 'to clothe or endue with attributes, qualities, or a character' or 'to clothe with or in the insignia of an office; hence, with the dignity itself' (*OED*)). From a later vantage-point, *Speech! Speech!* proposes that Hill's creative abilities may have been invested in 'proprieties'. The word 'proper', together with its cognates, are indeed key concepts in his work, invariably carrying a heavy load of irony, notably in 'September Song' (where 'the proper time' registers the obscenity of well-organized genocide), and in 'The Songbook of Sebastian Arrurruz': 'For so it is proper to find value/ In a bleak skill' (sect. 1, *KL* 53); 'cypresses shivering with heat (which we have borne also, in our proper ways)' ('A Letter from Armenia', *KL* 60); 'new-mated/ Lovers rampant in proper delight' ('To His Wife', *KL* 62); 'To caress propriety' (sect. 11, *KL* 63). One source of this irony is Hill's sense that the idea of propriety carries a note of self-congratulation which is not 'proper'. The etymological root of 'proper' in the Latin *proprius* ('one's own, special, particular, peculiar' (*OED*)) is also relevant. 'The Songbook' meditates on forms of possession and loss (the words 'possess', 'possession' and 'dispossession', like the words 'proper' and 'propriety', echo through Hill's work): memory as both possession of, and estrangement from, the past; sexual relations as enactment of an unrealizable fantasy of total possession (of love and of another person); art as a means of possessing experience which may also distance it. Arrurruz has learned that one can be self-possessed, full of propriety in one's words and behaviour, at the cost of being dispossessed of the impropriety of passion and the otherness of what is not 'proper' to oneself (in the sense of not belonging to oneself). The idea expressed in section 6 of *Speech! Speech!*

that in the realm of the proper 'cost can outweigh reward' implies some rueful sense on Hill's part that his own prolonged wrestle with what is proper to poetry and with what poetry may properly address may have cost him too much. *Speech! Speech!* evokes a media culture in which the idea of propriety, in behaviour and especially in discourse, retains little meaning. Hill would like to rescue concepts such as propriety, decency and duty from their current fate as quaint outmoded ideas or dubious clichés, but is faced by the problem of audience reaction (which gives this volume its title and one of its dominant themes). Here that reaction appears as an ironic interjection: '(*applause*)'. The poet, it seems, is forced into the role of a jester, and can only 'gape or grin haplessly' in the face of the decline of certain values. Section 6 then returns explicitly to questions of subjectivity and poetic voice, the risks associated with the grand 'we' and no less with the confessional 'I':

> On self-advisement I erased
> WE, though I | is a shade too painful, even
> among these figures tying confession
> to parody (*laughter*).

Then, in one of those dazzling and dizzying shifts of direction which help to define the style of *Speech! Speech!*, section 6 turns to one of Hill's great themes, the tragic history of war. At the same time, this section comments on Hill's own technique of representing the past by adopting elements of past discourses or styles, a technique evoked here in terms of a musical metaphor, that of the period instrument:

> But surely that's
> not all? Rorke's Drift, the great-furnaced
> ships off Jutland? They have their own
> grandeur, those formal impromptus played
> on instruments of the period (*speech! speech!*).[40]

The section concludes with the return of what might be the appreciative voice of an audience, the 'antiphonal voice of the heckler', or the self-mocking voice of the poet continually questioning his own impulse to public utterance.[41]

Speech! Speech! is a work on a huge scale, despite being a relatively slim volume. Hill has not lost his ability to condense complex and multiple meanings into a few words, and when this is extended over 120 sections, each of twelve lines, the result is an epic (and mock-epic) journey through past and present, intellectual history and postmodern cultural landscape, as well as a reflexive, comic debate on the history of Hill's own poetry and its reception. Hill commented at a reading that the volume was in part 'an oblique threnody' (lament or song of lamentation) for Diana, Princess of Wales, and the mass mourning and media frenzy surrounding her death are alluded to in many parts of the sequence (for example in sections 22, 36, 61, 71, 93, 94).[42] Rather than being the central subject of the sequence, though, Diana's life and death seem to serve as an exemplary instance for Hill's vision of contemporary British culture, focusing issues such as voyeurism and the appropriation and manipulation by the media of collective feelings and opinion. No brief account can do justice to the poem's range, nor interpret more than a fraction of its lines. It looks both backwards and forwards. The way in which it revisits some of the words, themes, preoccupations, aesthetic issues and critical debates which have become associated with Hill's poetry over half a century give it the status of an apology in both senses: an acknowledgement of mistakes and a defence of principles. However, in the originality of its style, its new openness to the contemporary, and its increased dependence on humour and parody, together with allusions to film, music-hall and clowning (often subliminally or briefly present in Hill's earlier work, but here given more evident presence and more scope), it breaks new ground and opens up new possibilities for Hill's poetry, establishing his place as one of the finest poets of this century as well as the last.

2

History and Politics

'There is a land called Lost
at peace inside our heads.'
— Geoffrey Hill, 'Two Chorale-Preludes:
on melodies by Paul Celan' (*T* 35)

'those who do not understand history are condemned to
re-live it'
— Geoffrey Hill, paraphrasing George Santayana,
interview with Blake Morrison, 1980 (*NS* 213)

Few, if any, postwar poets have been so intensely concerned
with history as Geoffrey Hill. This is immediately evident
from the range of historical periods explored in his poetry, in
works such as 'Requiem for the Plantaganet Kings' (the title
alludes to a medieval dynasty on the throne of England), 'Two
Formal Elegies: For the Jews in Europe' (on the Jewish victims
of the Nazis), 'Funeral Music' (described by Hill as 'a commi-
nation and an alleluia for the period popularly but inexactly
known as the Wars of the Roses') (*T* 67), 'Locust Songs' (on
early and nineteenth-century American history), *Mercian
Hymns* (with its eighth-century co-protagonist, Offa), 'The
Pentecost Castle' (based on Renaissance Spanish poetic forms
and poems), 'Lachrimae' (built around Renaissance English
poetry and music), 'An Apology for the Revival of Christian
Architecture in England' (on English history, primarily nineteenth-century), *The Mystery of the Charity of Charles Péguy* (on
a French poet who died in the First World War), 'Scenes with
Harlequins' (on a Russian poet of the early twentieth century),
'De Jure Belli Ac Pacis' (about German conspirators against
Hitler), 'Churchill's Funeral'. Furthermore, these poems do not

merely view the past from the present, but in various ways seek to immerse themselves and the reader in the individual and collective sensibilities and experiences of other eras and cultures, even while retaining a sense of the otherness of the past.

For example, 'The Pentecost Castle', a series of fifteen short lyrics revolving around themes of loss, melancholy and longing, and mixing elements of sacred and sexual love, inhabits the religious sensibility and aesthetic practices of the Spanish Counter-Reformation. Many of the poems are translations, versions and free adaptations of lyrics from *The Penguin Book of Spanish Verse*; furthermore, the process of writing them, as Hill has described it, was one of initial inspiration by a piece of music, followed by a gradual immersion in the music, drama and poetry of the period. Hill describes being 'enthralled' by a harpsichord piece 'by the sixteenth-century Spanish composer Antonio de Cabezón, "Diferencias sobre el canto del Caballero"' and explains:

> I then discovered that the theme for these magnificent variations was a little folk tune which gave Lope de Vega the motif for his play *El Caballero de Olmedo* ... These two figures, Cabezón and Lope de Vega, were united by this tiny thread of folk song ... The words of the little folk song became the first lyric of the 'Pentecost Castle' sequence. (*VP* 91–2)

Not only was Hill inspired by his models to write 'in the manner of the period' (*VP* 92), this very procedure of composing through the works of others is based on the practices of those earlier artists: Cabezón's composition consists of 'variations' on an existing musical theme, and de Vega's play incorporates the words of an existing folk song. Also formally influential on the piece are two Spanish poetic forms of the Counter-Reformation: the *glosa* (originating around the late fourteenth century), in which a short stanza introducing a theme is followed by a series of stanzas, each explaining or 'glossing' the original lines, and each concluding with one of those lines; and the *contrahecha a lo divino*, in which love poetry is recast as sacred, 'religious parody, or the rewriting of profane literature in religious terms', based on the fact that 'nothing was thought inappropriate for transformation: in an age of faith there is no barrier between the profane and the divine: one can nourish the other'.[1]

In this context a comment which Hill made in a Channel Four interview is very revealing of his sense of his relationship to the past, especially to cultural traditions. Asked by Hermione Lee whether he found it necessary to use the same language for both secular and religious passions (especially in 'The Pentecost Castle'), he replied that 'it is now necessary because for centuries sacred writers have been using the language of secular love to express their visions and ecstasies. Because it was done so much, the two are now, I think, inextricably involved' (*BF*). Rather than wishing to express his own sensibility or age through a quest for new forms, Hill often seems committed to an exploration of literary, theological and cultural traditions, through a poetic exploration of the discourses peculiar to them. Yet this attention to tradition produces highly distinctive and original poetry. Hill's emphasis is on discovering meaning in language, an approach which is reflected in his comment about choosing subjects for his poetry – 'they choose me. By the time I realize I'm doing it, it has sort of already got me in its grip' (*BF*) – and his description of himself as a 'radically traditional poet' (*BF*).

Hill's treatment of history is closely connected to the somewhat controversial question of his political positioning. His only public statement of explicit political support has been to express his admiration for the nineteenth-century radical Tory tradition associated with Richard Oastler, which he described as 'something quite apart from what we now know as Conservatism', adding that 'Modern Conservatism, which is Whiggery rampant, could be beneficially instructed by radical Toryism, but of course won't let itself be. Conservatives conserve nothing' (*VP* 87).[2] The congruence between Hill's self-description as a 'radically traditional poet' and his interest in a form of 'radical Toryism' is suggestive, since both imply a wish to preserve values combined with a going back to roots (the etymological meaning of 'radical') in order to question, or to rediscover, lost values. To those wishing to place Hill in terms of the politics of the late twentieth (or early twenty-first) century, though, the comment offers only oblique assistance. Hill's ambivalent reputation as a poet (hugely celebrated by

44

some, ignored or denigrated by others) is very much connected to historical and political questions. Those who disparage his work tend to do so either on the grounds of its alleged excessive dependence on the poetic forms and aesthetic principles of the past, or by claiming that it tends to reactionary nostalgia.[3] These issues will be considered shortly in a discussion of 'An Apology for the Revival of Christian Architecture in England' (a poem which prompted a fierce debate on these matters), and some more recent poems from *Canaan*. First, though, to understand Hill's view of history and politics, we need to consider the role of time in his work, and his treatment of the idea of transcendence – that is, a movement outside time into an eternal or timeless space.

Most accounts of the development of twentieth-century literature from modernism to postmodernism give a prominent place to the questions of time and space, and there is wide agreement that changes in the perception and representation of time and space are important aspects of cultural change in the twentieth century. One influential view holds that modernism, while obsessed with time, tended to spatialize it, 'via the distilled instant or the flattened circle of recurrence', in an 'attempt to defeat transience, by bending it into pattern'.[4] Thus Joycean epiphanies, the 'timeless moments' in Eliot's *Four Quartets*, the compressed classical and historical allusions of *The Waste Land*, the cyclical theories of history in Yeats, all subdue time in one way or another: by compressing experience into an instant, by transforming the messiness and openness of history into a finished and perfected work of art, by detecting recurrent patterns in history or by transcending change through a spiritual or aesthetic vision of timeless unity. Postmodernism, in contrast, it is claimed, 'breaks from this by emphasizing the contingent flow of temporality at the expense of the atemporal stasis of metaphysics'.[5] In other words, postmodern poetry is likely to employ more loose, multi-generic forms of narrative, to be open to change and contingency, to operate within the flow of time and to accept the unfinished, unperfected nature of human experience.

As so often when one considers Hill's work in the light of critical formulations of postwar cultural and literary change, that work is highly suggestive in relation to these ideas of the modern and the postmodern, but also reveals the limitations of such schemes by lying athwart supposedly distinct categories. Hill is a poet for whom the aspiration to transcendence and the sense of the poem as finished, perfected object are clearly crucial. Thus in an important early essay, 'Poetry as "Menace" and "Atonement" ', he proposes that 'the technical perfecting of a poem is an act of atonement, in the radical etymological sense – an act of at-one-ment, a setting at one, a bringing into concord, a reconciling, a uniting in harmony' (*LL* 2), and quotes two poets of the modernist era: Yeats's sense of the moment when 'a poem comes right with a click like a closing box' and Eliot's vision of completion as a form of mystical transcendence: 'when the words are finally arranged in the right way – or in what he comes to accept as the best arrangement he can find – [the poet] may experience a moment of exhaustion, of appeasement, of absolution, and of something very near annihilation, which is in itself indescribable'.[6] Hill himself has spoken of 'the authority of the right, true poem' (*BF*). Yet for Hill the appealing simplicity of the idea of poetry as atonement can only be 'ideally' his theme (*LL* 2); it must in practice be shadowed by the 'menace' of guilt and error which must be confronted in the recalcitrance of language itself, and not evaded through a gesture, such as Eliot makes, *beyond* language towards inexpressible truth:

> In the essay 'Poetry and Drama' Eliot speaks of 'a fringe of indefinite extent, of feeling which we can only detect, so to speak, out of the corner of the eye and can never completely focus . . . At such moments, we touch the border of those feelings which only music can express'. As Eliot well knew, however, a poet must also turn back, with whatever weariness, disgust, love barely distinguishable from hate, to confront 'the indefinite extent' of language itself and seek his 'focus' there. In certain contexts the expansive, outward gesture towards the condition of music is a helpless gesture of surrender, oddly analogous to that stylish aesthetic of despair, that desire for the ultimate integrity of silence, to which so much eloquence has been so frequently and indefatigably devoted.[7]

The relevance of this to Hill's vision of history will be apparent if it is set alongside lines from the second poem of 'Funeral Music', in which the voice of a fifteenth-century knight, reflecting on violent death in the Wars of the Roses, imagines a reconciliation or atonement of experience outside history, in related terms of music and silence:

> (Suppose all reconciled
> By silent music; imagine the future
> Flashed back at us, like steel against sun,
> Ultimate recompense.)

> (*KL* 26)

This vision (bracketed like the self in 'September Song') is immediately followed by an evocation of temporal and physical reality, and in particular the immitigable temporal reality of death:

> Recall the cold
> Of Towton on Palm Sunday before dawn,
> Wakefield, Tewkesbury: fastidious trumpets
> Shrilling into the ruck; some trampled
> Acres, parched, sodden or blanched by sleet,
> Stuck with strange-postured dead. Recall the wind's
> Flurrying, darkness over the human mire.

> (*KL* 26)

Hill's turning back to language from the lure of transcendent imaginings is paralleled by his turning back from imagined escapes out of history to the contingency and uncertainty of human experience within time. Hill's intense awareness of the otherness of the past and future makes his poetry less an expression of the desire to subdue time than a commentary on that desire. This is in part a matter of Hill's own historical and literary position after Eliot. Hill's perception that 'The dead keep their sealed lives/And again I am too late' ('Tristia: 1891–1938', *KL* 38) precludes an Eliotic sense that 'history is a pattern/ Of timeless moments'.[8] But it is also a matter of Hill's greater scepticism and reflexive self-questioning. Schematic historical accounts of modernism and postmodernism tend to separate out according to era what may rather be differences of mode (as some theorists of postmodernism have suggested), and Hill's poetry explores the tension existing, in various historical periods and literary sensibilities, between the impulse to transcendence and perfection and the sense of inescapable contingency. Throughout 'Funeral Music' a belief in, or longing for, forms of transcendent, eternal being and knowledge, are juxtaposed with the uncertainty, fear and unpredictable fate of the human body and mind. Images of a perfected, timeless world are questioned, criticized or contrasted with physical conditions, the existential uncertainty and harsh facts of human existence, reaching a climax in the last poem, where images of eternal harmony are confronted with the messy unpredictability of death:

> so we bear witness,
> Despite ourselves, to what is beyond us,
> Each distant sphere of harmony forever
> Poised, unanswerable. If it is without
> Consequence when we vaunt and suffer, or
> If it is not, all echoes are the same
> In such eternity. Then tell me, love,
> How that should comfort us – or anyone
> Dragged half-unnerved out of this worldly place,
> Crying to the end 'I have not finished'.

(KL 32)

This sequence of eight (largely unrhymed) sonnets develops, in a historically specific contest, a profound meditation on the senses and the intellect, the material and the spiritual, death and ideas of the eternal. The poems explore the power of abstract ideas in human life whilst imaginatively realizing the quality of lived experience in a politically turbulent and violent time of English history. Specific persons and events are alluded to – the aristocrats whose dates of execution are recorded at the head of the sequence and the Battle of Towton, mentioned in the second poem – and Hill illuminates his sense of these, and of the period in general, in the short 'essay' appended to the poem. That essay also defines the sequence in terms of music and architecture rather than narrative. Hill states that he was 'attempting a florid grim music broken by grunts and shrieks', and alludes to Ian Nairn's phrase 'the ornate heartlessness of much mid-fifteenth-century architecture' (*KL* 67). While 'the sequence avoids shaping these characters and events into any overt narrative or dramatic structure', it may be described in terms of 'ornate and heartless music punctuated by mutterings, blasphemies and cries for help' (*KL* 67–8). We are thus directed by Hill away from a search for historical narrative towards a more formal emphasis (reflected in the formal structure of the sonnet sequence), which rather attempts to convey some sort of *Zeitgeist* and to reflect on certain philosophical and psychological issues. These issues concern the apprehension of two realms, one mortal, physical, bounded in time, and the other eternal, transcendent and spiritual. The sequence raises the question of whether the belief in a transcendent realm outside time is philosophically tenable (as Christian theology would hold), or whether it is an illusion, a mere psychological projection of need for meaning, consolation or detachment. This question is focused with particular intensity by the historical and cultural setting, which combined, as Hill's essay suggests, intense, visionary religious faith with brutal violence, often in the same person. What happens in 'Funeral Music' is not that historical forms of belief in the transcendent are undercut by a modern, sceptical voice. Rather, impulses of faith and scepticism intertwine in various consciousnesses, which themselves meet and separate. Metaphorical ambiguities render up mystical and sceptical senses simultaneously. For example, in the second sonnet, 'we are dying/ To satisfy fat Caritas' (*KL* 26) reads two ways: our deaths are in the noble cause of caritas (Christian love), or, we are simply *dying* (in the colloquial sense of longing) to satisfy our own political ambitions (the literal Latin meaning of 'caritas' is 'scarcity of money' or 'high price', while 'fat Caritas' suggests the modern phrase for the excessively wealthy, 'fat Cats').[9] Yet 'Funeral Music' is far more moving than such a description might suggest, finding room for moments of individual tenderness, sadness and longing, as personal voices emerge from the 'heartless music' of the times:

> My little son, when you could command marvels
> Without mercy, outstare the wearisome
> Dragon of sleep, I rejoiced above all –
> A stranger well-received in your kingdom.
> On those pristine fields I saw humankind
> As it was named by the Father; fabulous
> Beasts rearing in stillness to be blessed.

49

The world's real cries reached there, turbulence
From remote storms . . .

                                        (sect. 6,   *KL* 30)

Here the innocence and intense imaginative activity of childhood provides an alternative, more humanly welcoming vision
of an 'other world', a temporary, fragile but precious refuge
from 'the world's real cries'. By the use of voices which seem
to shift between and at times blend, twentieth-century and
fifteenth-century perspectives, Hill gives a continuing relevance to this duality of worlds.

The historically distant setting and seemingly abstruse
concerns of 'Funeral Music' probably meant that, despite its
concern with questions of power and violence, critical responses to it did not focus to any great extent on political
issues. The situation was very different in the case of 'An
Apology for the Revival of Christian Architecture in England',
where the focus on nineteenth-century history (including the
history of the British Empire) and the sense of loss which
pervades much of the poem made contemporary political
implications more evident. This sonnet sequence (which deploys conventional sonnet rhyme patterns, though including
many half-rhymes) is indeed pervaded by a sense of loss and
the fading of past landscapes and ways of life:

It is the ravage of the heron wood;
It is the rood blazing upon the green.

                ('An Apology', sect. 1, 'Quaint Mazes', *T* 22)

The pigeon purrs in the wood; the wood has gone;
. . .
above this long-sought and forsaken ground,
the half-built ruins of the new estate.

                ('An Apology', sect. 11, 'Idylls of the King', *T* 32)

Critics of Hill's politics would point to such passages as
evidence of a cultural nostalgia, a reactionary hankering for the
supposed certainties of a hierarchical 'organic' community.
However, the sequence as a whole, whilst mourning losses,
consistently acknowledges the oppressions and injustices of
the past, and the relative nature of nostalgic constructions of
historical truth.

Issues of history, politics and poetry in this poem, and Hill's work more generally, were sharply raised by a debate in the *London Review of Books* during 1985–6, following a bitterly hostile review, by Tom Paulin, of a collection of critical essays on Hill's work. Paulin accused Hill of possessing an imagination which was not merely conservative but 'essentially *Blut-und-Boden*' – a German phrase meaning 'blood and soil' and associated with Nazi propaganda. Hill's poetry, Paulin claimed, was parasitic in its images upon that of T. S. Eliot, and was flawed by 'kitsch feudalism' and 'Tennysonian ... stagnant vowel music', the last of these particularly in the poem 'Idylls of the King' from 'An Apology'. He attempted to link a critique of the poem's rhythm (which he claimed was monotonously iambic) to a critique of Hill's poetry in general as nostalgic and reactionary.[10] As various critics demonstrated in the exchange of letters that followed, Paulin's review worked as much by abuse as argument and his claim of rhythmic monotony was not borne out by the evidence of the text.[11] Paulin also attributed guilt by association rather wildly: Hill was influenced by Eliot and so must share Eliot's politics; in *Mercian Hymns*, Hill had quoted a phrase, adapted from Virgil, which had also been adapted by the conservative politician Enoch Powell in a notorious racist speech, so (Paulin seemed to assume) Hill must also share Powell's politics. This last assumption seemed particularly imperceptive on the part of Paulin (a poet himself), since the allusion to the Tiber 'foaming' with blood, which Powell had used as an apocalyptic forecast of the supposed risks of immigration into Britain, was used by Hill in a hymn (*MH*, hymn XVIII) which is explicitly a reflection on the abuse of political power, on torture, sadism and voyeurism. If indeed any allusion to Powell was intended, such an allusion would hardly be complimentary.

Nevertheless, despite the wildness and inaccuracy of Paulin's critique, it articulated in extreme form an unease which many readers felt, and continue to feel, about the political implications of Hill's view of history. Paulin's view of Hill as a 'chthonic nationalist', conveying 'the idea of a mythic traditional religious England threatened by collectivist ideas' has at least superficial plausibility.[12] If, as I shall argue, such a view is ultimately a misunderstanding of Hill's complex position, it is nevertheless a view which most politically concerned readers of Hill will want to consider. In its title, epigraphs and allusions, 'An Apology' evokes a range of thinkers and writers who advocated, in various ways, hierarchical and authoritarian conceptions of cultural value, with specific reference to ideas of English culture. A brief account of some of the works and writers evoked may help to set the context for a discussion of the political implications of Hill's sequence.

Pugin's work of architectural and social criticism, *An Apology for the Revival of Christian Architecture in England*, argues that 'the venerable form and sacred detail of our national and Catholic architecture' ought to be adopted 'on consistent principle ... on authority ... as the expression of our faith, our government, our country'. He celebrates the traditional life of the rural community as he imagines it, based around the church and manor house, and deplores houses built in supposedly foreign architectural styles, such as 'bastard Italian, *without one expression of the faith, family or country of the owner!*'[13] The passage by Coleridge from which the first epigraph to the sequence is drawn distinguishes between 'the spiritual, Platonic old England' of 'Sir Philip Sidney, Shakspere [sic], Milton, Bacon, Harrington, Swift, Wordsworth' and the 'commercial Great Britain' which Coleridge associates with empiricist philosophers, politicians, and the poet Pope, and which he feels is alien to his own sensibility.[14] The second epigraph, from Disraeli's novel *Coningsby*, invokes a reinterpretation of English history which was consciously motivated by a political programme, that of the 'Young England' movement of the 1840s, which the novel was written in order to promote, a form of Radical Toryism which 'belongs to the same strand in nineteenth-century English thought as Coleridge and Carlyle, the romantic, conservative, organic thinkers who revolted against Benthamism and the legacy of eighteenth-century rationalism'.[15] The seventh poem of the sequence is entitled 'Loss and Gain', an allusion to a novel of religious conversion by Cardinal Newman, which argues for the ultimate suspension of private judgement in favour of religious authority.[16] An editor of *Coningsby* links Disraeli's Young England movement with Pugin's 'quest for spiritual values in medieval forms, such as Gothic architecture', and compares both with 'other contemporary crusades against the age, such as [Newman's] Oxford Movement'.[17] Hill's verdict on modern conservatism as 'Whiggery rampant' which 'conserve[s] nothing' (quoted earlier) echoes a comment by the eponymous hero of *Coningsby*: 'before I support Conservative principles ... I merely wish to be informed what those principles aim to conserve'.[18] Furthermore, the term 'Whig' (somewhat anachronistic in the late twentieth century) is also used (negatively) by Hill in attributing to his first four books: 'a sense of history (neither "Whig" nor Marxist) and a sense of place (neither topographical nor anecdotal)'.[19] Hill's use of the term recalls the dominant spokesman for organic conservatism in twentieth-century literature, T. S. Eliot, who uses 'Whiggery' as his term of abuse for the person who follows the 'Inner Voice' and rejects 'the existence of an unquestioned spiritual authority outside himself'.[20] The last line of 'Quaint Mazes' is, as Hill's note tells us, indebted to a review in the *Listener*. The phrase, and much of the review, are concerned with the destruction of religious icons during the reign of Edward VI – a loss of symbols which were part of patterns of communal belief. The author connects such patterns to the English landscape:

> what did the ordinary parishioner feel as the rood blazed upon the green and the whitewash blotted out the saints? He was illiterate but not without wisdom. His learning, his art and his religion were interwoven with intuitions and beliefs which were connected with the natural forces belonging to the few miles of field and woodland in which he was likely to spend nearly every day of his brief existence.[21]

Like those parts of the work of Pugin, Disraeli and Eliot which have been mentioned, this passage assigns a spiritual and moral significance to the relationship with the land.

Thus Hill's sequence evokes, through a whole series of allusions – Pugin, Coleridge, Disraeli's anti-Whig rhetoric, iconoclasm – a strand of organic, romantic conservatism which looked to the past for models and stressed authority and tradition. The question is to what purpose it does so. Hill's own defence against the charge of nostalgia has been made on several occasions, and is worth quoting in some detail; primarily he implies that his purpose is to analyse, not endorse, that way of thinking. Asked by Blake Morrison whether he would accept the presence of 'a sense of loss and nostalgia' in 'An Apology', he replied:

> I would, provided we can agree that the loss and nostalgia we're talking about in that sequence are for the most part England's ... We have got to get away from the supposition that if such emotions and experience as nostalgia and loss are the subject of a poem, or a sequence of poems, they must inevitably and necessarily be the nostalgia and loss of the poet himself. (*NS* 213)

He also asserted strongly the importance of such attention:

> I think that it is a tragedy for a nation or people to lose the sense of history, not because I think that the people is thereby losing some mystical private possession, but because I think that it is losing some vital dimension of intelligence ... I think my sense of history is in itself anything but nostalgic, but I accept nostalgia as part of the *psychological* experience of a society and of an ancient and troubled nation. (*NS* 213)

To John Haffenden, he suggested that:

> There are ... good political and sociological reasons for the floating of nostalgia: there's been an elegiac tinge to the air of this country ever since the end of the Great War. To be accused of exhibiting a symptom when, to the best of my ability, I'm offering a diagnosis appears to be one of the numerous injustices which one must suffer with as much equanimity as possible. (*VP* 93)

One likely riposte to this was made by John Lucas during the *London Review of Books* debate: 'To continue to worry at the matter of "Platonic England" ... is surely to demonstrate an addiction'; 'although Hill may say he is using nostalgia, in fact nostalgia is using him'.[22] Lucas adduced two specific arguments for this second claim: that in 'An Apology' 'nostalgia is identified through a particular, heavily allusive language, which is certainly *not* the language of society in its widest sense', and that 'what Hugh Haughton calls Hill's "fraught anachronisms", and correctly identifies as pastiche, become ways of warding off the kinds of criticism that are independent of nostalgia'.[23] Defences of Hill (including his own in the *New*

Statesman interview) generally allude to certain phrases in 'An Apology' which imply the oppressive aspects of British political and social history: 'in conclave of abiding injuries' (4, 'A Short History of British India (I)', *T* 25); 'The alien conscience of our days is lost/ among the ruins and on endless roads' (5, 'A Short History of British India (II)', *T* 26); 'Platonic England grasps its tenantry' (7, 'Loss and Gain', *T* 28); 'the mannerly extortions, languid praise,/ all that devotion long since bought and sold' (9, 'The Laurel Axe', *T* 30); 'Weightless magnificence upholds the past' (11, 'Idylls of the King', *T* 32). Lucas quotes two such phrases, but objects that they 'are unable to break free from the heavy layers of allusion and echo in which the sonnets are cocooned, which the phrases' own literariness endorses, and which the sonnet form itself in this case underpins'.[24] In response to Lucas's claim that Hill is really being used by nostalgia, Eric Griffiths retorted that 'Hill's remark accepts that one is used by what one uses', and in response to his specific points argues that 'there is no such thing as "the language of society in the widest sense" ' in a multilingual society such as Britain and that 'pastiche is one way of recognising this fact', and queries the assumption that allusions are something from which poetry needs to break free.[25]

If one sets aside the elements of personal abuse and the merely rhetorical debating points which marred sections of the *London Review of Books* debate, what emerges are two different models of poetry and its relationship to its subject, specifically here to the past. In one, adopted by Paulin and Lucas, the poet takes up a stance outside the subject matter of the poem, deploying the language of his or her own time to make explicit judgements on that subject matter. The words of the poem, although they may deploy irony, are essentially seen as the utterance of the poet, as his or her opinion, even if indirectly stated. In the opposing model, championed in various ways by Martin Dodsworth and by Griffiths, the poet writes from *within* the subject matter, inhabiting it and being inhabited by it, using its language to varying degrees, exploring the attitudes, mood and preoccupations of a particular ideology, tradition or historical period. The poem is less the utterance of the poet than something which the poet shapes out of the linguistic and cultural material found to hand within a particular cultural field. The difference is closely connected to the issue of impersonality raised in chapter 1: Hill sees himself as diagnosing elements of culture, not primarily as expressing his own feelings or views.

The debate is not one which can be conclusively settled, since it revolves around these two competing conceptions of poetry, as well as around various complex literary, cultural and political allegiances, so that the reaction of readers will depend partly on their own political views. There is much evidence to support Hill's claim that nostalgia for imagined organic pasts remains a potent force in parts of British culture, even as we enter the twenty-first century, if one thinks of attitudes to the royal family, hostility to diminution of British 'sovereignty' in Europe, the continuing popularity of historical costume drama on film and television, and the importance of images of war and empire in British self-representation (differences between England, Wales, Scotland and Northern Ireland are significant here: Hill's title refers only to England, it is worth noting). On the other hand, one might concede to Hill's opponents that the poet seems to have a particular intellectual and temperamental fascination with certain aspects of the past which others may see as of diminishing significance; if this makes him especially skilled in their evocation, it will not be an evocation to everyone's taste. However, the claim that 'An Apology' offers a critical analysis of nostalgia can be supported by a closer look at the final sonnet. First it is worth noting the characteristic ambiguity of the title of the sequence. While Pugin was using the word 'apology' in its old sense of defence or justification, Hill's use of the word in the 1970s is necessarily tainted by the modern sense of the word (an apology for something embarrassing or mistaken) and by the colloquial sense (in which 'an apology' for something is an inadequate attempt or substitute). Hill frequently puns on formal/ archaic and modern/ colloquial senses of a word in this way. Here the ambiguity means that Hill both does and doesn't apologize for reviving issues which may seem to some antiquated or archaic, and introduces an ironic, self-deprecating comment on what the poem can achieve.

The thirteenth and final poem of the sequence, 'The Herefordshire Carol', begins equally ambiguously:

So to celebrate that kingdom: it grows
greener in winter, essence of the year;
the apple-branches musty with green fur.
In the viridian darkness of its yews

it is an enclave of perpetual vows
broken in time. Its truth shows disrepair,
disfigured shrines, their stones of gossamer,
Old Moore's astrology, all hallows,

the squire's effigy bewigged with frost,
and hobnails cracking puddles before dawn.
In grange and cottage girls rise from their beds

by candlelight and mend their ruined braids.
Touched by the cry of the iconoclast,
how the rose-window blossoms with the sun!

('An Apology', sect. 13, 'The Herefordshire Carol', *T* 34)

In the first line, 'that kingdom' is both England and the imagined 'lost kingdom of innocence and original justice' to which Hill has alluded in interview (*VP* 88), and, while Hill might wish to link the two, he does not indulge the illusion that they have ever been historically one. 'So to celebrate' implies the ambivalent nature of the celebration which the sequence has offered. The fictional, mythologized realm of 'Platonic Old England' is 'an enclave of perpetual vows/ broken in time': history has been a perpetual breaking of the imagined perpetual promises of justice. This is a poem of self-consciously false representations, which ironically offers itself as kitsch prophecy (the harmless nonsense of *Old Moore's Almanac*): a squire who is only an effigy (with an ominous suggestion of violent protest – the burning of an effigy); a wig which is frost (or a squire who is a rather frosty Whig); an ideal realm which is 'greener in winter' because it is a kitsch 'evergreen' or because its beauty is musty.[26] Shrines, which figure devotion, are disfigured; stones are gossamer: 'All that is solid melts into air' (in the famous phrase of Marx and Engels) in this postmodernist meditation on lost ideas of lost certainties which were never there in the first place.[27] There is indeed a strong element of pastiche here, used as a way of registering the gap between nostalgic fantasies and material and social realities. Whether such critique through pastiche is, as John Lucas would have it, a way of pre-empting and resisting less sympathetic, more dismissive critiques, must remain an open question. The concluding image of the poem (and of the sequence as a whole) analyses the psychology of cultural nostalgia. It presents the glory of an Anglican heritage (figured by a magnificent stained-glass rose window, such as are found in English cathedrals) as coming to life (blossoming like a real rose) most intensely in the moment of threatened or impending destruction by the 'iconoclast'. The implication seems to be that a sense of an ideal beauty belonging to the cultural past is in part a product of the processes of loss and change. Hill's concluding word on 'Platonic Old England', then, is that 'Its truth shows disrepair'. 'An Apology' evokes, not a Platonic unchanging truth or ideal realm from which contemporary culture has fallen away, but a complex sense of the meanings attached by contemporary culture to such a myth of the past.

Hill's book-length poem of 1983, *The Mystery of the Charity of Charles Péguy*, shows elements of a postmodernist sense of the constructed and relative nature of historical accounts. It is less a poem about the life of Charles Péguy than one about the processes of historical and biographical myth-making, of which Péguy's life and associated events form an example. The title suggests an attempt to penetrate the mystery of the French poet's character and actions, but in fact the poem conspicuously fails to do so. Although the 'mystery' of Péguy is raised a number of times, the poem turns aside from it:

> But what of you, Péguy, who came to 'exult',
> to be called 'wolfish' by your friends? The guilt
> belongs to time; and you must leave on time.
>
> (M, 4.7)

> So, you have risen
> above all that and fallen flat on your face
>
> among the beetroots, where we are constrained
> to leave you sleeping and to step aside
> . . .
>
> to turn away and contemplate the working
> of the radical soul –
>
> (M 4.8–5.2)

The first passage above, referring to the question of Péguy's possible role in inciting the murder of the socialist deputy Jean Jaurès, seems evasive in its word-play, in its uneasy shift from 'The guilt/ belongs to time' (the guilt belongs to the past, or a version of the cliché 'history will judge'?) to the mock command, 'you must leave on time'. The second passage explicitly states that the purpose of the poem is more general and philosophical than biographical. Hill is perhaps rejecting as futile the quest for an essence of character or the ultimate truth of an individual's life. The poem keeps refusing to answer questions, proffering rhetorical (and hence unanswered) questions. In section 1, the directly posed questions of 1.4 ('Did Péguy kill Jaurès? Did he incite/ the assassin?') are followed by an intricate, shifting word-play around the phrase 'stand by', followed by a further rhetorical question ('Would Péguy answer . . .?'). In section 2, Péguy is present only in the form of his statue 'in blank-eyed bronze', while in section 3 the reader is seduced by a masterly evocation of a mythologized French countryside where, it is implied, the ideal or essential Péguy might be found ('here is your true domaine', M 3.5), only to find the quest ending in a closed door: 'bid the grim bonne-femme/ defend your door: "M'sieur is not at home."' (M 3.10). Sections 4 and 5 invoke the turning away described above, section 6 is about Dreyfus and history, and when Péguy reappears in 7, it is only to vanish again, in a passage which links lines of First World War infantrymen with the lines of the poem:

> The line
> falters, reforms, vanishes into the smoke
> of its own unknowing;
>
> (M 7.7–7.8)

In the last stanza of section 8, Péguy is ironically urged forward: 'En avant, Péguy!' But this urging, which might be a call to come forward and be recognized, is rather an urging forward into battle, and thus into death. The section concludes:

> The irony of advancement. Say 'we
> possess nothing; try to hold on to that.'
>
> (M 8.7)

This seems to serve as ironic advice to the reader. Section 9 is not primarily concerned with Péguy, while in the concluding section 10 it is again the physical reality of his death which is dominant, as 'he commends us to nothing' (*M* 10.4): 'Take that for your example!' (*M* 10.11).

As suggested by all these meta-textual gestures (in which the poem turns back on itself or us, commenting on its own procedures, ironically addressing the reader, etc.), this is a poem which constantly foregrounds the relationship between event and representation, whether that representation be literary, cinematic, sculptural or pictorial. The peculiar quality of the poem, the way in which it combines vivid evocation with a certain detachment from what it evokes, arises from its persistent merging of historical and biographical event with forms of discourse on, or representation of, that event. This continues, and further develops, the techniques of 'An Apology'. The equivalent to the ironized 'Platonic England' of 'An Apology' are the 'shaky vistas of old France':

> J'accuse! j'accuse! – making the silver prance
> and curvet, and the dust-motes jig to war
> across the shaky vistas of old France,
> the gilt-edged maps of Strasbourg and the Saar.
>
> (*M* 10.9)

The fist which strikes the table, sending the dust-motes travelling across the map in a parodic representation of the movement of generals' flags (themselves representations of troops), implicates the motivation of the war with the repercussions of the Dreyfus affair, including anger and guilt ('gilt-edged' as guilt-edged), and with economic forces ('silver'; 'gilt-edged' again, suggesting the stock market).[28]

In section 1 we find history portrayed, first as a race (with an ironic reflection on the pre-war belief in progress, and on the arms race), and then as a tragic farce:

> Crack of a starting pistol . . .
>
> History commands the stage wielding a toy gun,
> rehearsing another scene. It has raged so before,
> countless times; and will do, countless times more,
> in the guise of supreme clown, dire tragedian.
>
> (*M* 1.1–1.2)

The starting pistol suggests the assassination of Archduke Ferdinand at Sarajevo, which triggered the start of the First World War, while the image of history as manic director or ham actor plays on questions of historical determinism: who has written the script? The alleged repetitiveness of history is associated with the repetition of a play rehearsal (*répétition* means rehearsal in French); later in the section, film is also used to stress recurrence. The third stanza alludes to Shakespeare's *Julius Caesar*, a work full of reflections on violence and the rhetoric of violence, and the relationship between the two:

> In Brutus' name martyr and mountebank
> ghost Caesar's ghost, his wounds of air and ink
> painlessly spouting.

> (*M* 1.3)

Hill's lines recall Antony's repeated use of Brutus's name in his speech inciting the crowd, but it is hard to be sure whether Caesar is martyr and Brutus mountebank, or Brutus martyr and Antony mountebank.[29] Hill transfers these uncertainties onto Péguy: was he a dangerous inciter of war and violence, or a martyr to conviction? The 'wounds of air and ink' are both the rhetorical wounds of violent speech and writing, and the gaping holes and darkening blood of real wounds. Blood figures in *The Mystery* as wine (*M* 1.1), ink (*M* 1.3) and beetroot juice (*M* 2.9). Hill's vision of historical and political processes, though informed by aspects of the epistemological scepticism of postmodernism, retains a firm hold on the reality of suffering and the priority of the ethical.

Ethical concerns are more evidently focused on current political issues in parts of *Canaan* (1996). The first poem in the volume, 'To the High Court of Parliament', is unusually direct in its political satire, attacking corruption, cronyism and cynicism in British parliamentary politics of the 1990s. 'Where's probity in this . . .?', the poem asks, citing the elevation to the House of Lords of supporters of the government in power: 'the slither-frisk/ to lordship of a kind/ as rats to a bird-table?' (*C* 1). The poem is dated November 1994, at which time the 'cash for questions' scandal, questions about the expenses of cabinet ministers and the controversial proposal to privatize the Post Office were prominent in the British newspapers.[30] The poem might provide some support for those

61

who see Hill as hankering after an idealized national past, since the lines 'privatize to the dead/ her [England's] memory', while alluding to the Conservative government's selling-off of national industries and public assets at reduced prices (and the sale, for £1, of a Westminster graveyard), seem to imply a cheapening of the memory of England's past, a selling-off of that memory to the dead, as the living choose to forget. However, the lines might simply form part of Hill's critique of the forgetting of history as the loss of 'some vital dimension of intelligence' (*NS* 213), which need not imply that the past was ideal, or even better than the present, but only that we should strive to learn from it and to respect that within the past which is worthy of respect.

The poem is the first of a spaced sequence of three, each headed with the same title and date, at the beginning, near to the middle, and at the end, of the volume *Canaan*. The second of the three also contains sharply satirical metaphors and comparisons for those prominent in the contemporary public and political sphere, and presents that sphere as marked by hypocrisy, servility and corruption: 'your right ranters/ proud tribunes, place-men,/ shape-shifting nabobs'; 'knee-/ puppets jerked to riposte' (*C* 51). The biblical passage referenced at the top of the poem (Amos 3:8–11) prophesies divine punishment on those 'who store up violence and robbery in their palaces' (Amos 3:10), and begins with the verse: 'The lion hath roared, who will not fear? the Lord GOD hath spoken, who can but prophesy?' (Amos 3:8). The implication would seem to be that Hill's poem should be read as the utterance of a contemporary prophet, echoing Old Testament denunciations of corrupt and degenerate practices. The third poem of the same title alludes to a series of historical addresses to, criticisms of, or satires upon, the English parliament:

TO THE HIGH COURT OF PARLIAMENT
November 1994

– who could outbalance poised
                    Marvell; balk the strength
of Gillray's unrelenting, unreconciling mind;
grandees risen from scavenge; to whom Milton
                    addressed his ideal censure:

(*C* 72)

These lines seem themselves a sort of 'ideal censure' of the English parliament in history, juxtaposing the scathing but ambiguous allusion to 'grandees risen from scavenge' (noblemen who have achieved their rank by scavenging; or, who have risen from scavenge as from a feast; or, even, who have somehow risen *above* scavenge), with the ambivalent tributes of earlier artists. Marvell, whose own stance in certain poems is notoriously balanced, 'poised' or equivocal in relation to the shifting political allegiances of the English Civil War and the Restoration, wrote in his poem on Cromwell, 'The First Anniversary of the Government Under His Highness the Lord Protector', of 'they, whose nature leads them to divide,/ Uphold, this one, and that the other side'. What sounds at first like an image of division becomes an image of stability as the poem continues:

> But the most equal still sustain the height,
> And they as pillars keep the work upright,
> While the resistance of opposed minds,
> The fabric (as with arches) stronger binds,
> Which on the basis of a senate free,
> Knit by the roof's protecting weight, agree.[31]

James Gillray (1757–1815), a caricaturist, attacked the abuses of parliament and the royal family in a later century, while Milton's 'ideal censure' alludes to the poet's famous tract, *Areopagitica* (1644), against proposed censorship of book publishing by parliament, in which Milton exhorts the 'Lords and Commons of England' to 'consider what Nation wherof ye are, and wherof ye are the governours: a Nation not slow and dull, but of a quick, ingenious, and piercing spirit'.[32] The 'who' with which Hill's poem begins would seem, then, to be parliament itself, and the second, concluding stanza of the poem – which forms the final lines of *Canaan* – seems to confirm Hill's equivocal view of parliament, as embodiment of an ideal to which it remains inadequate:

> None the less amazing: Barry's and Pugin's grand
> dark-lantern above the incumbent Thames.
> You: as by custom unillumined
>   masters of servile counsel

Who can now speak for despoiled merit,
          the fouled catchments of Demos,
as 'thy' high lamp presides with sovereign
equity, over against us, across this
densely reflective, long-drawn, procession of waters?

                                 (C 72)

On the one hand this continues the vein of direct satire noted in the earlier poems of the same title. Even if the language is ornate, the implication of 'the fouled catchments of Demos' is clear enough: Demos being the people, or commons, and catchments the places where water collects, it is a metaphor for the soiling of the democratic processes by corruption; by 'despoiled merit' (another of those images of plunder, like 'scavenge' and 'rats to a bird-table') and the machinations of power ('servile counsel'). On the other hand, the passage registers a lyrical appreciation of the physical presence of the Houses of Parliament (Barry and Pugin being their principal architects), their setting on the Thames and, hence, to some degree, a cherishing of the symbolic political value which that institution holds in some eyes. A description of this as equivocal must be subject to Hill's own earlier rejection, as a description of his poetry, of the term 'equivocation', for which he took the dictionary definition of 'using words in a double sense in order to mislead' (VP 90). However, 'equivocal', though related to 'equivocation', need not carry the implication of misleading, but can mean 'having different significations equally appropriate or plausible; capable of double interpretation; ambiguous' (OED). This seems more appropriate to the poems, and more in accord with Hill's own formulation: 'It may be that the subjects [of my poetry] present themselves to me as being full of ambiguous implications . . . The ambiguities and scruples seem to reside in the object that is meditated upon' (VP 90). In other words, it is the political and ethical nature of parliament which is equivocal, rather than Hill's attitude to it.

    Some would see this as an attempt on Hill's part to avoid taking a political and ethical stance; he himself, it would seem, claims it rather to be a responsible fidelity to the complexity of the world, a refusal to simplify. If one accepts the latter view, one is left with the question of tone and voice, and what these imply about the role of the poet. Certain elements in these poems – the tone of denunciation, the allusion to the book of Amos – strongly suggest a vatic or prophetic element. This is also evident in the sequence entitled 'Churchill's Funeral' and in the volume title and epigraph, alluding to the worship of false gods by the children of Israel in the land of Canaan ('I wil euen destroy thee without an inhabitant').[33] Furthermore, the front cover of the Penguin edition uses an apocalyptic woodcut of buildings tossed around by flood waters. There is therefore an implication that the volume is to be read as a form of prophetic critique of the public sphere in England as the millennium approached, and it seems tinged with the apocalyptic mood of the fin-de-siècle. The role of an Old Testament prophet seems at odds with a poetic which abnegates polemic in favour of an exploration of the ambiguities inherent in things. But is Hill really adopting such a role? Certainly some critics seem to think so: Peter Sanger suggests the possibility of 'reading Hill's words ... as essays in poetic justice and prophecy'; Peter Firchow argues that 'even though the speaker of the elegy for Aleksandr Blok promises that he "will not deal/ in the vatic exchanges," ... the voice behind these poems is very much in the know about the dreadful doom that awaits the land of Canaan (for Canaan read Britain or Europe generally)'.[34] Harold Bloom, himself one of the most vatic of critics, goes furthest in proclaiming Hill 'the central poet-prophet of our augmenting darkness'.[35] On the other hand, Marcus Waithe argues that:

> Hill's determined scrutiny of prophetic utterance usefully challenges recent attempts to locate *Canaan* within a vatic tradition. His long-standing interest in visionaries and martyrs is of course well-documented, but it need not indicate a devotion to prophetic poetry, or an attempt to reproduce it himself.[36]

A partial answer may lie in those reflexive, self-critical gestures noted in chapter 1, in which Hill's earlier poetry rebuked its own impulses. It may be that *Canaan* both adopts a vatic tone *and* subjects that tone to sceptical, ironical scrutiny. Returning to the third of the poems 'To the High Court of Parliament' (C 72), we may see signs of this in the poem's strange and self-conscious use of pronouns. It begins surprisingly, with the word 'who', though preceded by a dash. At first we may be unsure whether this 'who' is an interrogative or a relative pronoun, and only after eight lines, a series of phrases in ambiguous apposition, do we reach a full stop which confirms the latter. Going back, we realize that we could read the title as part of the poem: 'To the High Court of Parliament – who could outbalance poised Marvell', so that the poem *addresses* parliament, though one may hesitate over the choice of 'who' rather than 'which' for an institution. In line 8 we find an equally ambiguous second-person pronoun: 'your mirth'; and in line 11 a syntactically isolated one: 'You: as by custom unillumined/ masters of servile counsel'. This 'you' seems almost an interjection or colloquial exclamation of reproach. Then, in line 13, we encounter another 'Who' at the start of a sentence, which we may be tempted to take, on analogy with line 1, as a relative pronoun, continuing the series of phrases and epithets applied to parliament. But, at the very end of the poem, we reach a question mark, indicating that this time the 'Who' was indeed an interrogative, so that the poem ends with an unanswered, indeed probably a rhetorical, question. Meanwhile, in line 15, the scare quotes around 'thy' in the phrase ' "thy" high lamp' seem to ask what would be an appropriate way to address such a thing as parliament, being a collection of people, a historical institution, a constitutional entity and a set of buildings, all at once. Since a prophetic stance is to a large extent defined by a mode of address, usually to a collectivity such as a nation or a people, the deliberate uncertainty and oddness in the process of addressing someone or something in this poem seems to register the problems of a late twentieth-century prophetic voice.

These questions may be illuminated by reference to 'Churchill's Funeral'. This is a poem of five sections written in unrhymed, short-lined quatrains, with significant use of alliteration (smoke-stained glass, sect. I, C 43), assonance ('Innocent soul/ ghosting for its lost/ twin', sect. II, C 45) and enjambment ('where she entertains/ the comedians', sect. III, C 47). Another notable feature is the use of the repeated word: 'its whole shining/ history discerned/ through shining air' (sect. II, C 45); 'simply as of right/ keep faith, ignorant/ of right or

66

fear' (sect. II, C 46). The title of the sequence would seem to announce an elegy for Britain's famous wartime prime minister, whose funeral took place in 1965, almost three decades before the publication of this sequence in Hill's *New and Collected Poems* (1994) (prior to its appearance in *Canaan*). There are many images of the Second World War, but the sequence makes little direct allusion to Churchill himself, reading rather, as Peter Sanger suggests, as 'a Blakean, prophetic vision of the causes and consequences of the collapse of post-Second World War London into moral and physical desolation'.[37] Sanger's description raises again the question of whether Hill plays off the present against a past seen as superior. Certainly Hill seems to believe strongly that both World Wars called forth sacrifices by many ordinary people, to which contemporary memory and contemporary society fail to do justice, as he argues in his 1985 interview:

> I think that tribute should be paid where tribute is due – I think that if the previous generations, as we're sometimes ritualistically told they did ... died that we might live, then from time to time one thinks we're not worth their sacrifice ... [in the First World War] something very decent was torn out of the heart of English society; English learning was torn out, English moral consciousness, a great deal of it, was torn out – the great common people of this country had the heart torn out of them in the slaughter of those Pals battalions, and it seems to me something that must not – must *not* – be forgotten – it must be remembered with gratitude. And the anger, as I say, flares up from time to time when one considers some of the social evils, the cruelty, the injustice, the sheer thoughtless mayhem of our time, and one thinks, was it for *this* that they died – and I think that one must honour decency and sacrifice. (*BF*)

It is a theme he returns to thirteen years later, in section XXVI of *The Triumph of Love*.

But does Hill impute moral and physical superiority to pre-war or wartime London, and present himself as a prophet denouncing decline and decadence? The ambiguous, oblique, gnomic style makes it hard to be certain, but surely the allusions to Blake, Eliot and Elgar would suggest that the corruption detectable in contemporary London is a perennial condition. 'Churchill's Funeral' begins with an epigraph drawn

from 'a note by Elgar on the original inspiration for his
Overture *Cockaigne'* (*C* 75): '. . . one dark day in the Guildhall:
looking at the memorials of the city's great past & knowing well
the history of its unending charity, I seemed to hear far away in
the dim roof a theme, an echo of some noble memory . . .' (*C* 43).
The jaunty, populist optimism of the *Cockaigne* overture, Elgar's
later associations with naive English nationalistic pride, and the
sentimental, misty tone of Elgar's quoted comment all suggest
an ironic use of this quotation, and this is supported in the final
stanza of the first poem, where the 'noble melody' is reduced to
a recollected tune, hummed or whistled:[38]

> *nobilmente* it
> rises from silence,
> the grand tune, and goes
> something like this.
>
> (*C* 44)

William Blake is a strong presence in this sequence, as
indicated by the epigraphs to sections III and V. Elgar's
utopian, selective memory of the 'unending charity' of the City
of London is surely to be seen as rebuked by Blake's two
poems entitled 'Holy Thursday' (in *Songs of Innocence* and
Songs of Experience respectively), and his 'London' (in *Songs of
Experience*). Read as a pair, the 'Holy Thursday' poems evoke
and then demolish a melioristic view of charitable institutions:

> Is this a holy thing to see
> In a rich and fruitful land –
> Babes reduced to misery,
> Fed with cold and usurous hand?

When the *Innocence* 'Holy Thursday' is reread in the light of
these bitterly satirical lines from the *Experience* 'Holy Thursday', its vision of charity children entering and singing in St
Paul's acquires more apocalyptic overtones: 'Till into the high
dome of Paul's they like Thames waters flow'. Blake's 'London' is similarly dystopian and apocalyptic:

> I wander through each chartered street
> Near where the chartered Thames does flow,
> And mark in every face I meet
> Marks of weakness, marks of woe.[39]

Hill's opening phrase, 'Endless London', picks up on, while at the same time rendering ambivalent, Elgar's 'unending charity', but it also alludes to the idea of the 'eternal city', which in T. S. Eliot's poetry becomes one pole in a dualistic representation of London:

> the 'imperialistic Eliot' is the poet of the Roman *'urbs aeterna'* . . . the other side of this city is the Babylon of the Apocalypse. Eliot knows that 'behind the temporal disaster of Babylon ... the timeless pattern of the eternal city must survive'.[40]

Does the timeless vision of the eternal city underlie Hill's apocalyptic visions of wartime and postwar London, the 'sirens, laughter,/ the frizzed angels/ of visitation/ powdered by the blast' (sect. III, C 47), the 'blitzed/ / firecrews, martyrs/ crying to the Lord,/ their mangled voices/ within the flame' (sect. IV, C 48), and the 'vandals of sprayed blood' (sect. V, C 49)? 'Endless' has a more ambivalent ring than 'timeless', suggesting also appallingly vast (as London can easily seem) and tediously long-drawn-out, and it thus drags the transcendent, imagined 'timeless' London back into the realm of commerce and empire, including Conrad's vision of London (in *Heart of Darkness*) as the dark heart of the imperial horror. Rather than endorsing the myth of the ideal city, Hill may imply that the ideal city is a tempting but politically dangerous fantasy. Such points of interpretation are very difficult to settle with any confidence, because of the highly ambiguous way in which meanings are constructed in this sequence.

Perhaps Hill's sense of his own poetry as often misunderstood may have contributed to a willingness, in *The Triumph of Love*, to be at times more direct about his view of British history, as in the following lines attacking the British government's policy of appeasement during the rise of Hitler:

> Last things first; the slow haul to forgive them:
> Chamberlain's compliant vanity, his pawn ticket saved
> from the antepenultimate ultimatum; their strict
> pudency, but not to national honour; callous
> discretion; their inwardness with things of the world;
> their hearing as a profound music
> the hollow lion-roar of the slammed vaults;
>
> (*TL*, sect. X)

Some of the same themes are evident here as in 'Churchill's Funeral' – questions of national honour, the dubious motives of those in power, and the corrupting effect of financial interests ('the slammed vaults' being presumably those of banks) – but both the precise historical events alluded to, and the poet's attitude to those events, are clearer. In contrast to the unanswered 'who can judge of this?' in section II of 'Churchill's Funeral' (C 46), these lines do assume the right to judge. Probably few would now dissent from Hill's disapproval of appeasement, but the opening line seems to involve the poet taking upon himself a large responsibility: why should it be his role to forgive the errors of the statesmen of his childhood? Those who regard Hill as habitually arrogating to himself an inflated role as prophet and judge would no doubt see this as further proof of hubris, but it may be that Hill simply feels so intensely about the events of the twentieth century that the need to try to forgive is, for him, a psychological necessity. Furthermore, it may be a mistake to assume that Hill speaks in his own person here, any more than he does in section CXXXVIII, where the guilt of the survivor is expressed through the voice of a supposedly cowardly participant in the First World War, saving his skin at the expense of famous artist victims of that conflict, the composer George Butterworth and the poet Edward Thomas.[41] Such adoption of fanciful personae is part of the vein of tragi-comic clowning in the sequence. Alongside a certain directness, *The Triumph of Love* is notable for the humour which, always present in Hill's work but frequently subdued, now finds freer expression, and it is to this element in his work that Hill himself points in response to accusations of excessive vaticism:

> the harshest critics of *The Triumph of Love* seem not to notice what I might call a very strong element of autobiographical comedy, or even clownishness; they say that Hill claims for himself the status of a prophet, and nobody has the right to make such a claim in the late twentieth century, and that there is something disgusting in seeing a writer describe on the same level the Shoah, the First and Second World Wars and his petty resentments. And all I can say is that no such claim is made by the author . . . The whole structure of the sequence, particularly the way phrases are shaped, the way

70

certain allusions are made to Laurel and Hardy, and comic papers is an acknowledgment of this monstrous inequality. (*PR* 284–5)

Ultimately *The Triumph of Love* affirms a conception of poetry, not as prophecy or satire, but as a formal, aesthetic mode of consolation:

> what are poems for? They are to console us
> with their own gift, which is like perfect pitch.
> Let us commit that to our dust. What
> ought a poem to be? Answer, *a sad*
> *and angry consolation.*

(TL, sect. CXLVIII)

This sense of form as consoling is enacted in the way the sequence itself concludes with a final, one-line section, echoing the opening one-line section (though with a tiny change). This framing line represents a poignant aesthetic image from the poet's childhood, rather than a political or moral point: 'Sun-blazed, over Romsley, a livid rain-scarp' (*TL*, sect. I); 'Sun-blazed, over Romsley, the livid rain-scarp' (*TL*, sect. CL).

Disagreements over the political implications of Hill's poetry seem likely to continue, given the complexity and ambiguity of his style. However, part of the answer may be that Hill conceives of the relationship to history in primarily ethical rather than political terms. Whereas Joyce's Stephen Dedalus sought to wake from the 'nightmare' of history, Hill seeks rather to reawaken his reader's sense of that nightmare.[42] Another clue lies in Hill's essentially Christian and theological imagination, which disposes him to think in terms of what Walter Benjamin called 'Messianic time': 'an authentic, redeemed historical time [which] is only possible at the end of history with the advent of the Messiah'.[43] Yet Hill combines this with a high degree of epistemological scepticism (doubt as to the availability of truth and knowledge). This combination, which will be discussed in chapter 3, means that Hill frequently evokes images of history patterned in terms of enduring Christian archetypes and a purposeful development of the world according to divine plan, but subjects such images to a postmodern sense of the relative and discursive nature of constructions of time and history, and the loss of belief in grand narratives.[44] Although Hill has evident preoccupations

71

and areas of interest, and offers at times strong words of praise or blame, his poetic technique of working from within historical discourses, rather than judging them from outside, makes it all but impossible to define a single position for him.

3

Faith and Doubt

'a heretic's dream of salvation expressed in the images of
the orthodoxy from which he is excommunicate'
                    – Joseph Cary, quoted by Geoffrey Hill
                                in interview (*VP* 98)

There can be no doubt about the importance of religion,
specifically of Christianity, to Hill's poetry, yet it would be
misleading to describe him as being, in any straightforward
way, a religious or Christian poet. The quotation which heads
this chapter, and which Hill invoked, in characteristically
oblique manner, to comment on his sense of his own relationship to belief, emphasizes above all exclusion. It conjoins both
the willed exclusion of the heretic, who chooses to follow his
own beliefs outside the current orthodoxy, and the imposed
exclusion of the excommunicate, cast out by the edict of church
leaders. In the history of the Catholic Church, of course, the
two have often been the same, excommunication being a
penalty for what the Church has judged to be heresy, which
may or may not have been willed as such. The implication of
Hill's use of this quotation is perhaps that he himself has such
a relationship, not so much to orthodoxy, as to faith itself; that
faith, or at least secure faith, is something which represents an
unattainable dream for him, and from which he is excluded,
though whether by choice or external determination it is
impossible to say. Such uncertainty makes sense: presumably,
while faith can be willed, it cannot necessarily be willed
successfully. Biographical speculation on this point would be
inappropriate, but certainly Hill's poetry can often be read in
terms of a lost dream of faith, confronted and undercut by a

highly sceptical intelligence. One consequence of this ambivalent stance is that critical responses to Hill often seem conditioned in a specific and marked manner by the beliefs and opinions of the critic: critics sympathetic to Christian belief will often stress the elements of transcendence, mysticism and vaticism in the poetry, while more secularly minded critics emphasize its scepticism, instability of meaning and self-mockery. Hill, then, is a poet for whom Christian modes of thought are central. This is reflected in the importance to his poetry of Christian symbols (such as the cross), concepts (such as redemption), narrative paradigms (such as the Fall), and texts (theological, devotional and poetic). Elements of these occur in many of his poems, whatever the subject, but certain poems from throughout Hill's career address matters of faith and doubt more explicitly: from *For The Unfallen*, poems such as 'Genesis', 'God's Little Mountain', 'The Bidden Guest', and 'Canticle for Good Friday'; from *Tenebrae* the sequences 'The Pentecost Castle', 'Lachrimae' and 'Tenebrae'; from *Canaan*, 'Psalms of Assize', 'De Anima', 'Whether the Virtues are Emotions', 'Whether Moral Virtue Comes by Habituation' and 'That Man as a Rational Animal Desires the Knowledge Which is His Perfection'; certain sections from *The Triumph of Love*. The present chapter will focus on a number of these poems.

'Genesis', which stands at the beginning of both *For the Unfallen* and *Collected Poems* and reworks the myth of creation and Fall from the Old Testament into a meditation on the imaginative act of creation, is frequently interpreted as an account of Hill's own beginnings as a poet:[1]

> Against the burly air I strode
> Crying the miracles of God.
>
> And first I brought the sea to bear
> Upon the dead weight of the land;
> And the waves flourished at my prayer,
> The rivers spawned their sand.
>
> (FU 15)[2]

However, to identify the speaker of the poem with the poet would imply an unreasonable hubris. If the poem is instead read in the light of Coleridge's idea of the Primary Imagination as 'a repetition in the finite mind of the eternal act of creation in the infinite I AM', it emerges as a mythologization of the imaginative act, drawing on the Romantic link between imagination and creation.[3] As Harold Bloom suggests, 'Genesis' follows the example of Blake in imagining the Creation and the Fall as the same event.[4] Since imaginative perception is also, in Romantic terms, a form of creation, this implicates perception with man's fallen state (whether this is taken in a dogmatic sense as a state of sin, or, more metaphorically, as the state of subjective and contingent knowledge dictated by our involvement in what we perceive). Thus the Romantic view of perception, when combined with a Christian sense of man's fallibility, assimilates creativity and error, figured by the Creation and the Fall. The poem also refers to the Incarnation and the Crucifixion ('There is no bloodless myth will hold'), and the Last Judgment ('The bones that cannot bear the light'), and thus touches on the Christian archetypes which are persistent paradigms in Hill's poetry. Similarly, 'The Bidden Guest' is built around pentecostal imagery. In 'Genesis' both the Crucifixion and the Incarnation are suggested by the lines:

> Where Capricorn and Zero cross,
> A brooding immortality –

> (FU 16)

The zodiac sign of Capricorn is associated with the element of earth, so its intersection with zero is an appropriate symbol of the paradox of incarnation, the intersection of the earthly and the eternal (zero implying the absolute otherness of the eternal).[5] In his discussion of the absolute qualitative difference between God and man, eternity and time, the theologian Karl Barth envisages Jesus as the 'undimensional line of intersection' and, quoting Kierkegaard, states that 'Jesus as the Christ, as the Messiah, is the End of History'.[6] In Christian eschatology Christ is the end of history in two senses: the fulfilment of its purpose and, at his second coming, its cessation. He is also its beginning, since he is one with the creator, and since the year of his birth is given the designation of zero in the Christian calendar.

In Hill's poetry the Incarnation is not only a paradigm for the paradoxical relation of the worldly and the eternal, but also stands for a mode of apprehension of experience: a mode which combines spiritual concerns and high intellectual abstraction with sensuous immediacy and powerful physicality. In the last line of 'Canticle for Good Friday' the paradoxical nature of the Incarnation, its combination of eternal design with physical contingency, is condensed in the puns on 'issue' and 'congealing': 'Creation's issue congealing (and one woman's)' (FU 39). The same sense of the bloody reality of Christ's sacrifice, and a concomitant ambivalence about the Christian dispensation, are expressed in the final stanzas of 'Genesis':

> By blood we live, the hot, the cold,
> To ravage and redeem the world:
> There is no bloodless myth will hold.
>
> And by Christ's blood are men made free
> Though in close shrouds their bodies lie
> Under the rough pelt of the sea;
>
> Though earth has rolled beneath her weight
> The bones that cannot bear the light.
>
> (FU 17)

The second line quoted states the paradox in the Christian view of suffering: what appears in worldly terms to be ravaging is, in eternal terms, redemption. But the next line turns the stanza into a statement, not about the way things are, but about the way we understand them; not 'the world' but the 'myths' by which we live (including the myth which the poem itself seeks to create). This line also retrospectively modifies the sense of 'By blood we live'. The references to the Last Judgment in the poem are contained in an oblique biblical allusion (a frequent feature of Hill's poetry): 'For behold, the Lord cometh out of his place to punish the inhabitants of the earth for their iniquity: the earth also shall disclose her *blood* and shall no more *cover her slain*' (Isaiah 26:21). The italicized words here inform the imagery of the fifth section of 'Genesis' (the next chapter of Isaiah contains a reference to Leviathan, which is mentioned in 'Genesis'). Isaiah 26 and 27 prophesy the Last Judgment, and promise bodily resurrection. The latter is perhaps the doctrine that renders the reconciliation of faith and ordinary experience most difficult, so this allusion is an appropriate culmination to the ambivalence expressed in section V of 'Genesis' about the Christian myth of blood sacrifice.

'Genesis', then, mythologizes the activity of the ordering human imagination manifesting itself in Promethean attempts to control the world. The consonance and assonance which link 'strode' ('Against the burly air I strode') with 'strove' ('The tough pig-headed salmon strove') acknowledge the pig-headed element in this activity (an early instance of the humour concealed in Hill's puns). In sections III and IV the imagination turns to the making of unworldly spiritual myths, but in V is brought back to the physical body which it inhabits and confronts the paradoxical and potentially dangerous nature of faith. The poem also considers the response of the imagination to violence: observing ('I stood and saw') or warning ('I cried: "Beware ..." '). In the treatment of these themes Hill's rhetorical power is already in evidence, but his technique is not as yet fully adapted to his concerns: both the use of an 'I' and the narrative structure based on the book of Genesis are somewhat misleading. They are really pseudo-structures: they provide a framework, but do not carry the weight of the meaning of the poem. It is neither essentially about a person (even an allegorical one), nor essentially about a sequence of events (even a mythical one). Of the other early religious poems, 'Canticle for Good Friday' also takes a biblical model, but this time from the New Testament, imaginatively reworking the story of Doubting Thomas, while 'God's Little Mountain' and 'The Bidden Guest' are mythic or metaphorical narratives of moments of faith and crises of doubt, with the Pentecostal tongues of flame as central images. All of these early poems are notable for the physicality of the images in which they convey spiritual and psychological experiences: 'The strange flesh untouched, carrion-sustenance/ Of staunchest love, choicest defiance,/ Creation's issue congealing (and one woman's)' ('Canticle for Good Friday', *FU* 39); 'And I was shut/ With wads of sound into a sudden quiet' ('God's Little Mountain', *FU* 18); 'And so my heart has ceased to breathe/ (Though there God's worm blunted its head/ And stayed.)' ('The Bidden Guest' *FU* 21).

In *King Log* and *Mercian Hymns*, though Christian terms and paradigms are still used (for example in the title of

'Annunciations' or the biblical imagery of 'History as Poetry'), the main focus is on historical, ethical and personal themes. Furthermore, in *King Log*, double meanings express an extreme tension between mystical impulses towards transcendence, and sceptical, satirical subversion of such impulses, producing the sort of self-revoking paradoxes (as in 'Annunciations') described in chapter 1. When Hill returns to more explicitly religious poetry in *Tenebrae*, he turns to European religious and devotional traditions as formal models, and this serves to effect a degree of reconciliation between sceptical and mystical impulses. As well as adopting rhetorical devices (such as the tradition of paradox in Christian devotional writing), Hill draws on other media (primarily music, which the poems both allude to and imitate), and the work of other artists (authors, composers, architects). The element of ritual is also important: Hill commented in an interview that '*Tenebrae* is a ritual, and like all rituals it obviously helps one to deal with and express states' (*NS* 213).[7] The result of these mediative processes is the creation of a framework which contains the contradictions and conflicts without effacing them, and a resultant emphasis on form or pattern. This displaces the conflict of mystical and sceptical modes onto the level of style, art or rhetoric; tension, resolution of tension, or the absence of resolution become elements of an aesthetic patterning analogous to musical structure.

The contrast between the radical fragmentation of Hill's poetry in the early sixties and the aesthetic patterning of *Tenebrae* may be illustrated by a comparison of forms of paradox from 'Annunciations' and from 'Lachrimae': 'Our God scatters corruption' ('Annunciations', sect. 2, *KL* 15); 'I founder in desire for things unfound./ I stay amid the things that will not stay' ('Lachrimae', sect. 5, 'Pavana Dolorosa', *T* 19). The former, as Hill himself has noted, yields two diametrically opposed senses and these senses belong to different world-views: that of militant Christian faith, and that of a sceptical critique of Christian institutions. It is possible for the reader to construct a link between them by taking one to refer to 'our God' as we (mortals) conceive him, the other to refer to God's true eternal nature, so that the overall sense would be something like: 'our worldly, self-interested idea of God is a source of corruption, but the true God we are unable to comprehend is a destroyer of corruption'. But such a reading feels very much like an ingenious attempt to harmonize ideas which remain in conflict in the poem. In the example from 'Lachrimae', the final lines of 'Pavana Dolorosa', the oppositions are elegant, ceremonious, melancholy, rather than disruptive. The words 'founder' and 'unfound' do not represent a logical contradiction, but a pleasure in the play of surface meaning; the line has the sound of a paradox without its sense. Similarly, in the last line the paradox of the stubborn persistence of the transient is separated out into an elegant antithesis between the speaker, who remains bound to the apparent solidity of worldly things, and the illusory nature of that solidity. The formal elegance of these lines is reminiscent of both Counter-Reformation devotional poetry and Petrarchan love poetry. In the *Tenebrae* volume a mediating role is played by Counter-Reformation works and modes, whether English or Spanish, literary or musical. The taste for paradox, punning, intricacy, formality, ceremony and reflexivity which is apparent in such works provides Hill with models and forms which embrace contraries with a formalistic harmony rather than a disruptive tension. In 1980 Hill commented that 'paradox, and the closely related oxymoron, belong both to the tradition of mystical poetry and to the tradition of Petrarchan poetry, which are the main models for "The Pentecost Castle" and "Lachrimae"' (*NS* 212). In the case of 'Lachrimae', Robert Southwell is a direct source, providing the epigraph to the sequence. The lines quoted from 'Pavana Dolorosa' may be compared with Southwell's 'Saint Peter's Complaint':

> I fear'd with life, to die, by death to live:
> I left my guide, now left, and leaving God.
> To breath in blisse, I fear'd my breath to give,
> I fear'd for heavenly raigne, an earthly rod.[8]

Here the paradoxes are gestures of (troubled) faith founded on Christian dogma, such as the paradox of death as the entrance to eternal life, and a life of sin as a form of death. In Hill's 'Lachrimae', faith and doubt co-exist, but the rhetoric of paradox within which Southwell works provides a means to the formal ordering of this conflict. Since the poems of Hill's volume interweave human and divine love, it is important that the poetic traditions on which he draws employ similar rhetorical effects for both forms of love. An example would be the death/ life paradox that appears in Spenser's *Amoretti* as part of a spiritual apotheosis of conjugal love: 'And if those fayle, fall downe and dy before her;/ so dying live, and living do adore her'.[9]

The epigraphs of 'The Pentecost Castle' and 'Lachrimae' help to define the preoccupations of these poetic sequences. Hill has stressed their importance, saying that 'the essential meaning of each sequence is contained in the very carefully chosen epigraphs to each of them' (*VP* 92), but this hardly conveys the complex and oblique nature of the relationship between epigraph and poem. The following are the epigraphs to 'The Pentecost Castle' (*T* 7): 'It is terrible to desire and not possess, and terrible to possess and not desire' (W. B. Yeats); 'What we love in other human beings is the hoped-for satisfaction of our desire. We do not love their desire. If what we loved in them was their desire, then we should love them as ourself.' (Simone Weil).[10] Yeats's dictum suggests a cynical hedonism, but also hints at the vanity of human wishes and the insufficiency of life to the demands of the soul. The worldly knowledge and the critique of merely human love implied by Yeats here echo similar statements, made with rather different intent, in seventeenth-century devotional writing, such as John Donne's observation in one of his sermons that 'to desire without fruition is a rage, and to enjoy without desire is a stupidity'. The sermon suggests how worldly pleasures may be converted into spiritual ones:

> so that soul, that hath been transported upon any particular worldly pleasure, when it is intirely turn'd upon God, and the contemplation of his all-sufficiency and abundance, doth find in God fit subject, and just occasion to exercise the same affection piously, and religiously, which had before so sinfully transported, and possest it.[11]

The Weil epigraph gives expression to the scepticism about ordinary behaviour and sentiments which arises from judging by rigorously spiritual standards. In *Gravity and Grace* Weil sets out a programme for the transcendence of such limited human desire, again recalling Donne's concerns:

We have to go down to the root of our desires in order to tear the energy from its object. That is where the desires are true in so far as they are energy. It is the object which is unreal. But there is an unspeakable wrench in the soul at the separation of a desire from its object.[12]

This idea that the energy of desire may be valuable, though the object be wrong, is matched in the Southwell epigraph to 'Lachrimae' (T 15): 'Passions I allow, and loves I approve, onely I would wish that men would alter their object and better their intent'.[13] Southwell's lines are an uncompromising demand for a life of faith and abnegation, masked by an apparent moderation of tone. 'Onely' carries the full weight of a turn in syntax which is also a complete reordering of life: the change, which Southwell requires of men, from ordinary human passions and loves, to the love of Christ. The obliquity of the relationship of epigraph to poem is evident in the ironic inversion of the first line of the Southwell epigraph in the first line of the fifth sonnet of 'Lachrimae' ('Pavana Dolorosa'): 'Loves I allow and passions I approve'. This inversion creates a more musical rhythm than Southwell's original words, and hints at a reconversion from the spiritual back to the sensual, a return upon that conversion or transcendence advocated by Donne, Southwell and Weil.[14] 'Pavana Dolorosa' evokes an idea of 'ascetic opulence': a sensual pleasure in abnegation and its rituals:

> Loves I allow and passions I approve:
> Ash-Wednesday feasts, ascetic opulence,
> the wincing lute, so real in its pretence,
> itself a passion amorous of love.

> (T 19)

'Ash-Wednesday feasts' plays on the verbal proximity of 'feasts' and 'fasts' to suggest, with a wry humour, that the individual drawn to the rituals of abnegation may 'feast' upon asceticism, like the Reverend Mother of 'Fidelities' ('An Apology', sect. 10), who 'breakfastless, could feast her/ constraint' (T 31). But 'Pavana Dolorosa' does not merely subvert the discourses of faith evoked by Hill's epigraphs; rather, it reinscribes the close parallels between spiritual desires and those of the flesh, noted by the authors of the epigraphs, in the

81

form of an intimate sense of the complicity between different forms of desire and satisfaction. However, the unmistakable note of satire in Hill's 'Lachrimae', directed at the self-indulgence which may lurk beneath devotional practice, does indeed go beyond his sources. 'Pavana Dolorosa' employs two compoundings of 'self' to suggest the difficulty, for devotional practice, of evading the demands of the self: 'Self-wounding martyrdom, what joys you have'; 'Self-seeking hunter of forms, there is no end/ to such pursuits'. These lines compare the 'self-wounding' martyr with the 'self-seeking' artist (the 'hunter of forms'), eliding their respective quests for a perfection, a completion, which is both part of, and apart from, the self.[15] The possibility of a narcissistic element in the vocation of the martyr is strongly implied in T. S. Eliot's poem 'The Death of Saint Narcissus' in which, as David Trotter writes, 'martyrdom seems like a continuation of narcissism by other means, a different and more ingenious way of tasting one-self'.[16] By linking martyr and poet in such terms as the above, Hill implicates the elegant patterning and achieved completion of the 'Lachrimae' sequence with the doubtful motivation which it postulates for 'self-wounding martyrdom'.

One source for the connection of aesthetic completion with martyrdom is section III of 'Little Gidding', from T. S. Eliot's *Four Quartets*, where we find the line: 'A symbol perfected in death'.[17] Many elements of 'Lachrimae' have a source in *Four Quartets* which, while containing contraries such as faith and doubt, hope and despair, lyricism and abstraction, builds up an idea of its own overall pattern as an image of harmony and reconciliation, with music as the primary model for this patterning. The traditions of religious discourse to which Hill's epigraphs point us, and which are otherwise evoked in 'The Pentecost Castle' and 'Lachrimae', share with Eliot this sense of complex, paradoxical relations of opposition and complementarity between worldly and spiritual, fleshly and ascetic. Donne (in certain poems), Lope de Vega (a source for 'The Pentecost Castle'), Saint John of the Cross (alluded to in 'The Pentecost Castle') and Southwell all worked within that tradition, which uses the language of sensuality for spiritual aspiration or vice versa. In his introduction to the *Tenebrae* volume, published in the *Poetry Book Society Bulletin*, Hill stated that 'many of the poems in *Tenebrae* are concerned with the strange likeness and ultimate unlikeness of sacred and profane love; and it is this concern which, perhaps, creates the dominant tone of this book'.[18] Here Hill's critical judgement of his own work tends to imply a more definite and unproblematic conclusion than a reading of the poetry itself suggests: the poems of *Tenebrae* leave unresolved the question of whether, ultimately, likeness or unlikeness are more to be emphasized. The fundamental dualities, between physical and spiritual, profane and sacred, worldly and transcendent, recall such earlier works as 'Annunciations' and 'Locust Songs', with their rhetoric of unresolvable paradox. But in *Tenebrae*, such duality is approached through an architecture of epigraphs, quotations and allusions, which form part of the mediating process to which I have referred. The formality, intricacy of structure and density of allusion in the *Tenebrae* volume can be seen as part of a process of reintegration of elements which had, in Hill's earlier poetry, remained in tense opposition.

The primary mediating presence of the first sequence in the volume, 'The Pentecost Castle', is the Spanish Counter-Reformation sensibility which Hill found in the work of the composer Antonio de Cabezón, and the poet and playwright Lope de Vega. Hill's description of the genesis of the sequence emphasizes a number of key elements for the *Tenebrae* volume as a whole, including process, envy of music, the iconic and hidden connections. Hill has described the evolution of the sequence in terms of a process of engagement with, and exploration of, the music and poetry of others (*VP* 91–2). This establishing of a link between his own work and other artists, other media, another age, involved, and was validated by, a tracing of earlier instances of such mediation: de Vega and Cabezón both worked on and through a folk song (the lyrics and the music respectively), and are thus, in Hill's words, 'united' by this 'tiny thread' (*VP* 92). The musical composition by Cabezón which Hill heard performed, 'Diferencias sobre el canto del Caballero', takes the form of variations ('Diferencias'), again a key word for the *Tenebrae* volume.

Hill's sequence joins in the creative procedures of de Vega and Cabezón, in that it elaborates the mood of the song while also incorporating a version of it (a translation of the song forming the first poem of 'The Pentecost Castle'). Hill told John Haffenden: 'I began to read my way into Lope de Vega's work – that play in particular' (*VP* 92), and his fascination may be explained by the combination of passionate lyricism, formality and sardonic humour found in *El Caballero de Olmedo*, all notable features of Hill's own poetry. The dominant mood of de Vega's play is, however, that of melancholy longing, and it is this mood that Hill develops in 'The Pentecost Castle'. A precedent for the conversion of sexual to spiritual is offered by a Counter-Reformation Spanish poetic form, the poem '*contrahecha a lo divino*', in which love poetry is recast as sacred. Lope de Vega was one of the practitioners of the '*contrahecha a lo divino*' poem, which has been described as 'religious parody, or the rewriting of profane literature in religious terms', indicating that 'in an age of faith there is no barrier between the profane and the divine: one can nourish the other'.[19] It is easy to see from such comments how important the mediating role of a Counter-Reformation sensibility might be for Hill, who is not living in an age of faith, and whose own relationship to faith seems so troubled and complex.

Poem 1 of 'The Pentecost Castle' takes from the Spanish song of de Vega's play the short lines which, with some variation, are to be the model for the sequence as a whole, but whereas the Spanish lines vary in rhythm and length (between five and eight syllables), Hill's version, in the first poem, is extremely regular, every line having four syllables, except for the repeated three-syllable phrase ('not to go') of the middle two lines of the middle stanza. Hill's verbal changes from 'Que de noche le mataron' heighten the repetitive, circular quality already present in the Spanish. The effect approaches that of pattern poetry; the visual appearance on the page of 'The Pentecost Castle' contributes significantly to the sense of its sparseness and lucidity, and distinguishes it sharply from the rest of Hill's poetry. Yet there is also an effect of enigmatic, allusive resonance. While the allusions to Medina and Olmedo are clear in the context of de Vega's play (since Alonso comes from Olmedo and has triumphed in Medina), in Hill's sequence they become enigmatic and atmospheric.

The result of Hill's translation and adaptation in poem 1 is an insistent, incantatory lyric, suggesting a dishonourable murder and implying that the victim may be a type of Christ. Strictly speaking, a type must be found in the Old Testament, but the concept of typology has a certain aptness here. Frank Kermode, discussing forms of modern typological thinking, identifies the danger, in the assumption that 'histories and fictions cannot avoid conforming with types', that such thinking may become 'sentimentally ritualistic and circular'.[20] This is certainly a risk in Hill's poetry, which revolves around Christian paradigms, such as the Crucifixion, the Incarnation and the Fall. Those suspicious of such aspects of Hill's work would be likely to point to the poems of *Tenebrae* as most open to the charge of embodying 'sentimentally ritualistic and circular' modes of thinking. The title of the volume announces its concern with ritual, and stylistically the volume is characterized by finely wrought, intricate patterning, rather than free flow or energy. Indeed, the whole manner in which Renaissance and Counter-Reformation forms and modes are used could be criticized as governed by a sentimentalizing typology. The non-specificity of 'The Pentecost Castle' in terms of narrative or event opens it to readings in terms of types. In contrast to 'Funeral Music', 'The Songbook of Sebastian Arrurruz' and *Mercian Hymns*, 'The Pentecost Castle' is not historically located, although its sources and stylistic mode may be historically locatable. This perhaps makes it liable to the 'unjustified archaism' which Kermode identifies as a temptation resulting from 'systematized typological insights'.[21] Hill, however, might respond that what may seem unjustifiably archaic to an uninformed modern sensibility can be defended as fidelity to a long and rich tradition – a tradition by which such a sensibility might be informed. At all events, the type or figure is an important concept for the *Tenebrae* volume, while in 'Lachrimae' the idea of figuration appears with musical and iconic connotations.

Poem 2 of 'The Pentecost Castle' continues the highly patterned effect of poem 1, using identical first and last stanzas (with the exception of the capitalized first letter). *The Penguin Book of Spanish Verse* provided models, more or less closely followed by Hill, for most of the poems of the sequence.[22] Poem 2, rather than corresponding closely to any one lyric from *The Penguin Book*, partakes of the mood of several, especially those anonymous poems of the fifteenth and six-teenth century that tell of a journey to a grove and a lovers' meeting, hinting at both pleasure and remorse or pain.[23] This second poem, and indeed the sequence as a whole, can be seen as developing from the first poem in the manner of musical variations, 'a form in which successive statements of a theme are altered or presented in altered settings'.[24] In 'The Pentecost Castle' literary themes (love, death, loss) and moods (melan-choly, longing) persistently recur, though modified by other elements. The absence of an overt narrative or story encour-ages the reader to seek structural principles in such elements.

The remaining poems of the sequence do not share the close syntactical parallels of poems 1 and 2. Nevertheless, there are sufficient continuities to sustain a broad parallel with the variation form, poem 1 acting as the model on which the variations are built. The structure of three quatrains remains constant throughout, as do the short lines of two or three stresses, with between four and seven syllables. The use of patterned repetition (with small changes) within a poem recurs in poem 11, and the pair of identical lines found in the second stanza of poem 1 is matched in the first stanza of poem 12. Running through the sequence are a number of chains, made up of verbal echoes or clusters of imagery, revolving around: trees, orchards and groves; death and wounds; darkness and light; the idea of a journey. In the absence of either an overt narrative or a clearly defined subjectivity within the sequence, the reader's strategy becomes one of listening to such structur-ing patterns, and building up around them a sense of theme, atmosphere, mood. This strategy makes the reader aware of patterns, without imposing an equivalence on the multiple strands of feeling and idea that are present. The sequence does not equate sacred and profane love, any more than it equates the sensibilities or philosophies which it evokes (such as those of Yeats and Weil). Rather, it articulates a patterned movement of interrelation between them.

While variation provides a model for 'The Pentecost Castle', the musical device of false relation plays a similar role in the next sequence in *Tenebrae*, 'Lachrimae, or Seven Tears Figured in Seven Passionate Pavans'. This device is an important element in John Dowland's composition for consort of viols (dated 1604, and dedicated to Queen Anne) from which Hill takes the title of his poem.[25] Diana Poulton writes of Dowland's *Lachrimæ* that 'suspensions, false relations, and the clash of parts moving against each other at temporarily discordant intervals are combined in a musical texture of extraordinary emotional intensity'.[26] False relation involves 'a chromatic contradiction between two notes of the same chord ... or in different parts of adjacent chords'.[27] Hill himself has used false relation as an analogy for a literary effect, describing a line from *Cymbeline* as 'the taming of "false relation" to a new constructive purpose', and adding that 'dissonance is the servant preparing the return of harmony' (*LL* 66). As a local, expressive use of dissonance between two parts, false relation provides an analogy for Hill's use of two or more conflicting strands of meaning, including dissonant puns. The first sonnet of 'Lachrimae', entitled 'Lachrimae Verae', centres on a paradoxical sense of connection with, and estrangement from, Christ.

> Crucified Lord, you swim upon your cross
> and never move. Sometimes in dreams of hell
> the body moves but moves to no avail
> and is at one with that eternal loss.
>
> You are the castaway of drowned remorse,
> you are the world's atonement on the hill.
> This is your body twisted by our skill
> into a patience proper for redress.
>
> I cannot turn aside from what I do;
> you cannot turn away from what I am.
> You do not dwell in me nor I in you
>
> however much I pander to your name
> or answer to your lords of revenue,
> surrendering the joys that they condemn.
>
> (*T* 15)

The duality between the true Christ and the speaker's comprehension of him is figured by two strands of reference, one to Christ himself, the other to a crucifix, icon of Christ's atonement. The latter strand has reflexive connotations, since Hill's sequence is itself a form of icon of Christ.

In the opening lines of the sonnet, the icon seems to swim before the eyes of the speaker, while Christ is imagined as a swimmer through the stream of time or history, an eternal being traversing an element not his own. There is also a sense of incongruity in the idea of Christ's outstretched arms as like those of a swimmer, a comparison which humanizes but diminishes, and suggests the uncertainty of the speaker's faith. While the icon seems to move in front of his eyes, swimming with tears, the contemplation of Christ fails to move the speaker to a firm faith, or a transformation of his life. 'I cannot turn aside from what I do' suggests both 'I cannot reform my life' and 'I cannot avoid contemplation of my own sins, nor responsibility for them'. Line 3 continues the punning on 'move', with the paradox that it is dreams of a hellish state (in which the body makes muscular contractions but, in the dream, is unable to run away) which bring the speaker closest to Christ, in terms of imagining his suffering on the cross. At the same time, the dream experience parallels the failure of the penitent, who is, in emotional terms, 'moved' by Christ but unable to change. Line 4, by its reference to the atonement ('at one'), emphasizes the paradoxical nature of the fleeting sense of closeness to Christ which the dream offers; that it is a closeness to an experience of loss or separation. 'Eternal loss' suggests both damnation and loss of faith. For both the unabsolved sinner, and the atheist or agnostic, the atonement offered by Christ is lost (in different senses).

In 'Lachrime Verae' there is a skewed or twisted quality to the metaphors of the poem which conveys the unease and guilt of the speaker, his sense of being at odds. The idea of Christ as swimmer is followed through, but the metaphor shifts uneasily: first Christ is a swimmer on his cross, then he is a castaway on an island, presumably to be identified with the hill of the Crucifixion. The relationship of 'castaway' and 'drowned remorse' is skewed, since a castaway is someone who, perhaps alone among his companions, escapes drowning. Here, however, Christ must be envisaged as 'cast away' on Golgotha either as a result of the 'drowning' of remorse, or in such a way as to rescue 'drowned remorse' by arousing repentance. Furthermore, the drowned remorse brings us back to the feelings of the speaker gazing at the crucifix, his remorse drowned by his swimming tears, or by his inability to move. Thus, while lines like 'You are the castaway of drowned remorse' flow smoothly as regards metre and sound, the metaphor is coiled into a baroque intricacy. The evocation of musical form in 'Lachrimae' serves to unify the dualisms of Hill's poetry by creating a meta-level of signification through the patterning of tension and conflict. An example of this occurs in the seventh sonnet, 'Lachrimae Amantis':

> What kind of care
> brings you as though a stranger to my door
> through the long night and in the icy dew
>
> seeking the heart that will not harbour you,
> that keeps itself religiously secure?

(T 21)

The main effect here is of harmonic dissonance between the two senses of 'religiously': 'in a scrupulous, conscientious manner' and 'in respect of religious practice'. The combined effect is both sharp self-condemnation (for scrupulosity exercised to protect selfish illusions) and an ironic reflection on the liability of institutionalized belief to be misused for such a purpose. A prominent feature of the sequence is oxymoron, which might be compared to false relation in adjacent chords (as opposed to the simultaneous notes of a pun). Examples in 'Lachrimae' include: 'celestial worldliness', 'slavish master' (sect. 2, 'The Masque of Blackness', *T* 16), 'harsh grace', 'void embrace' (sect. 4, 'Lachrimae Coactae', *T* 18), 'ascetic opulence', 'so real in its pretence' (sect. 5, 'Pavana Dolorosa', *T* 19).

'Lachrimae' can be read as an account of an individual's troubled relationship to Christian faith, its symbols and its demands. Earlier models are dominant: not only are Dowland and Southwell evoked as mediating presences, but the last sonnet is a free translation of a Spanish sonnet by Lope de Vega.[28] However, these elements can be seen as providing a supporting framework for the expression of an experience, by drawing on the creations of other artists with whom there is a shared aspect of sensibility. There is a reflexive strand in 'Lachrimae' that serves to associate the sequence with both the power and the vicissitudes of the icon (or sacred art object), of sacred objects generally, and of religious ritual. Reflexive doubt about the archaic and anachronistic aspects of the sequence as a twentieth-century literary work is indicated in the sixth sonnet, 'Lachrimae Antiquae Novae':

> Beautiful for themselves the icons fade;
> the lions and the hermits disappear.
> Triumphalism feasts on empty dread,
>
> fulfilling triumphs of the festal year.

(T 20)

The suggestion here of an empty triumphalism which has substituted the ritual of the Christian year for substantial faith must reflect some unease back on to the status of ritual and formality in *Tenebrae*. 'Beautiful for themselves' may troublingly remind us of the acknowledgement in 'September Song': 'for myself it/ is true', and contributes to that awareness of the persistence of the ego which has already been noted, and which is manifest in the phrases 'self-love', 'Self-wounding' and 'self-seeking'. This awareness is maintained in spite of the counterbalancing evocation of 'the decreation to which all must move' ('Pavana Dolorosa'), that abandonment of the self which Simone Weil asserts as the essential prelude to communion with God: 'Decreation: to make something created pass into the uncreated . . . God can only love himself . . . Our existence is made up only of his waiting for our acceptance not to exist'.[29]

The two musical analogies which have been suggested offer possible models of a relation to a cultural tradition. To write variations on pre-existing words or on a tune is to allow the original to inhabit one's own work, but to give it life within one's own creative process, so that the variation is an integrative, mediative form. Such a model of interaction may be used to distinguish Hill's allusiveness in *Tenebrae* from the model offered by T. S. Eliot's *The Waste Land*. The allusions of Eliot's poem remain fragments: the appropriate analogy for the structure is the mosaic or collage, the image of the sensibility of an age which experiences itself as fragmentary and hoards a fragmentary past. The poems of *Tenebrae* rather attempt to construct a modern sensibility as a variation upon a Renaissance sensibility. Here *Four Quartets* provides a model in its use of the English past. If *The Waste Land* offers us the poet in the imaginary museum of Western culture, lamenting the fragmentary collection, poor labelling, and his own enervated state, then in *Four Quartets* he has gone on a retreat and, despite his disclaimer that it is 'an occupation for the saint' to strive 'to apprehend/ The point of intersection of the timeless/ With time', such seems to be his project.[30] As I have already suggested, Hill's sequences in *Tenebrae* resist, to a greater degree than Eliot's work, the movement of temporal transcendence, the stepping outside time to evoke a vision of eternity, or the intensity of a timeless moment.

The second musical analogy, that of false relation, implies a postmodernist relation to the past, in that the verbal effects which may be characterized as forms of false relation express an awareness of cultural tradition which is not only self-conscious, but also highly ironic. The puns and oxymorons of 'Lachrimae' express the predicament of a modern sensibility deeply involved with past modes of thought and belief, but troubled by an awareness of this involvement with the past as fictional and constructed, 'real in its pretence', a false relation.

Whereas, in *Tenebrae*, borrowed formal patternings create a certain reconciliation between the warring impulses of faith and doubt in Hill's poetry, when he returns again to religious themes in *Canaan*, Hill uses verse forms which convey a certain hesitancy and doubt, though still with a powerful impulse to affirmation. In place of the elegant, melancholy symmetries of the lyric in 'The Pentecost Castle' and the balanced paradoxes of the sonnet form in 'Lachrimae', we find, in sequences and poems such as 'Of Coming into Being and Passing Away', 'De Anima', 'Ritornelli' and 'Psalms of Assize', largely unpunctuated free verse, with short lines (sometimes of a single word), intermittently 'stepped' (displaced from the left margin). (The volume does contain sonnets, as well as fourteen-line poems which John Taylor compares to 'ruins of classical sonnets', but these are poems on historical and political themes, such as the sequence 'De Jure Belli Ac Pacis', about the German conspirators against Hitler, or the third of the poems entitled 'To the High Court of Parliament'.)[31] Patterning on the page is again, as in 'The Pentecost Castle', important, but is suggestive less of symmetry and more of disturbance. The effect is of a questioning, exploratory and troubled monologue on devotional or theological topics, blurred and fractured by ambiguity and shifting syntax:

91

prodigal ever returning
darkness that in such circuits
reflects diuturnity
               to itself
and to our selves
               yields nothing
finally –

          but by occasion
visions of truth or dreams
as they arise –
          to terms of grace
where grace has surprised us –
the unsustaining
               wondrously sustained

          ('Of Coming into Being and Passing Away', C 4)

          unearthly music
given to the world
message what message
               doubtless
the Lord knows
when he will find us
               if ever
we shall see him
with the elect
               justified
          to his right hand

          ('Psalms of Assize', sect. II, C 61)

In the first passage quoted, the 'darkness' is presumably that of death, or absence of physical being, from which we emerge into life, and to which we return (hence 'ever returning'). The poem suggests the paradox of darkness that reflects, but reflects only its own persistence; the rare word 'diuturnity' (meaning 'long duration or continuance', *OED*), carries audible echoes of 'die', 'you' and 'eternity'. Uncertain visions of the eternal or unimaginably long stretches of time recur in Hill's work, from 'all echoes are the same/ in such eternity' ('Funeral Music', sect. 8, *KL* 32) to 'Endless London' ('Churchill's Funeral', sect. I, C 43), and are a part of a sensibility informed by eschatological visions. The unyielding nature of such long-lasting darkness (awaiting resurrection, or simply in a state of complete non-being) gives way only contingently ('but by occasion') to 'visions of truth' and 'terms of grace' – that mystery of grace which, according to Christian theology, is our only protection against the abyss of death. The poem ends with a characteristic feel of paradox, reminiscent of 'Lachrimae'. Bearing in mind that the meanings of 'sustain' include 'to keep in being' and 'to keep going' or 'carry on' (*OED*), it is presumably the human individual who is 'unsustaining' (can neither continue life nor maintain being), yet is 'wondrously' sustained by grace. Paraphrased thus, the poem seems an orthodox statement of faith, but the ambiguity produced by the lack of punctuation, together with the hesitancy of voice created by the verse patterning, render the actual effect of the poem more conflicted. In the second passage quoted above (from 'Psalms of Assize', section II) such ambivalence is more evident, via double meanings recalling those early compactions of 'Annunciations': here 'the Lord knows' might be pious faith or ironical, colloquial expression of doubt. 'Unearthly music' evokes the perhaps unique ability of music to convey intimations of the eternal and transcendent but, as always in Hill's work, the risk of illusion inherent in this process is confronted, as the register shifts from the seemingly calm, assured formality of 'unearthly music/ given to the world' to that of a troubled or even impatient colloquial questioning: 'message what message' (we hear, I think, an absent question mark). Hill's caution in relation to 'the expansive, outward gesture towards the condition of music' (in his comments on Eliot quoted in chapter 2) is felt here, in a strain of his work which goes back at least as far as 'Funeral Music', where an imagined reconciliation by 'silent music' is revoked by the sense that 'all echoes are the same/ In such eternity' (sects. 2 and 8, *KL* 26, 32). The last four lines of 'Psalms of Assize', section II (quoted above), acquire an ironical tinge from the preceding lines, and this is reinforced by the odd textual allusion in 'justified/ to his right hand'. These lines are displaced towards the right-hand side of the page; they are not (in the terminology of printing) 'justified' – indeed, poetry is in general not justified (so as to fill entirely the space from left to right margin) because line breaks in poetry are essential, not contingent. The textual displacement makes it inevitable that we will think of these technical senses of 'justified' and 'right hand' alongside the theological ones. To justify in the technical sense is 'to make exact; to fit or arrange exactly' (*OED*). This suggests, perhaps, the way in which artistic form, whether in music or poetry, can provide an image of perfection, and hence an image of the divine. The fact that the lines in 'Psalms of Assize' so notably do not 'fit exactly' implies a self-conscious inability to affirm the validity of such an image, thus returning us to the epigraph to the present chapter: the lines, read one way, offer a 'dream of salvation', but both the double meanings and the displaced lines suggest excommunication, or self-excommunication, from assured faith. The title of the sequence, 'Psalms of Assize', in itself of course suggests the musical, since psalms are sacred songs or hymns, but since 'assize' refers to some form of legal proceeding, the idea of the law and judgement is introduced (phrases such as 'The Great Assize' or 'The Last Assize' have sometimes been applied to the Last Judgment of Christian eschatology). The poems of the sequence carry Latin epigraphs drawn, as Hill's note tells us, from the marginalia of John Colet (a notable Christian humanist and reformist cleric of the late fifteenth and early sixteenth centuries) to the *Epistolae* (letters, but in this case effectively 'philosophical and theological essays') of Marsilio Ficino (an Italian humanist philosopher of the late fifteenth century).[32] Ficino was an important neo-Platonist, who translated Plato and was head of a Platonic academy in Florence, and so Colet's extensive marginal comments on his *Epistolae* represent an important moment in the reception of neo-Platonism in England. In using these epigraphs, Hill is therefore returning to some of the aspects of neo-Platonic philosophical debate which were evoked in 'Funeral Music', which alludes to the neo-Platonic belief that the world of eternal ideas or forms is apprehended by the intellect, while the inferior material world is apprehended by the senses. For example, the epigraph to 'Psalms of Assize' section II is concerned with the conflict between reason and intellect on the one hand, and the senses on the other. The epigraph translates as 'No man can serve both masters and go up and down at the same time; you have either to go up or go down'.[33] The two masters here are, first, 'reason and intellect', which 'rise toward the divine nature' and, second, 'taste and touch', which 'point downward' towards 'corporeal nature'.[34] As so often when Hill writes about intimations of the divine or transcendent, the example of T. S. Eliot is evoked, but dissented from; Colet's words here might be read as rebuking the too-easy mystical acceptance of Eliot's line from 'The Dry Salvages': 'And the way up is the way down, the way forward is the way back'.[35] The opening lines of Hill's poem take up these ideas in ambiguous, ironical ways:

> Ascend through declension
> the mass the matter
> the gross refinement
> > gravitas
> everlasting obsession
> vanity by grace

(C 61)

'Declension' means 'declining, or sinking into a lower or inferior condition' and 'deviation or declining from a standard; falling away (from one's allegiance), apostasy', but is more commonly used in its grammatical sense ('setting forth in order the different cases of a noun, adjective, or pronoun' (*OED*). The word thus introduces a further textual allusion into the poem. 'The mass' might refer to material weight or the Catholic mass, while 'the matter' might suggest either physical matter or a problem (as in the phrase 'what is the matter?'). The oxymoron of 'gross refinement' leads on to the ambiguity of 'gravitas', a Latin version of the word gravity, used as a term of approbation ('weighty dignity; reverend seriousness', *OED*), which can rather easily slide towards mockery ('staidness', *OED*). The word 'gravitas' also suggests, in this context, 'gravity', in the sense used by Simone Weil in *Gravity and Grace*, where it represents an inertial force in human nature ('Obedience to the force of gravity. The greatest sin');[36] also relevant are lines such as the following from section IV of 'De Jure Belli Ac Pacis': 'Evil is not good's absence but gravity's/ everlasting bedrock' (C 33), and Hill's own discussions of the gravitational or inertial pull of language.[37]

The paradoxical mode of thought favoured by mystics such as Weil (for example, 'we only possess what we renounce') lends itself to the poised yet shifting style of Hill's ambiguous meditation in 'Psalms of Assize'.[38] The nature of such mystical discourse is addressed specifically in section CXXV of *The Triumph of Love*, where we find, not so much a poetry of faith and doubt as a poetry of theological, logical and philosophical debate, mixed with humorous interjections and colloquial asides. In some ways this section covers similar ground to 'Psalms of Assize' (questions of truth and language, intellect and grace), but in a completely different poetic mode, one of expansive, humorous, almost relaxed debate, in place of the highly wrought, condensed asymmetries of the earlier poem. The sort of grammatical and spiritual double meaning attached to 'declension' in 'Psalms of Assize', section II, is here alluded to – 'Mysticism is not/ affects but grammar', while the bemused struggle of a modern poetry reader with Latin quotations (such as the epigraphs to 'Psalms of Assize') is voiced within the poem itself, by the interjection of the 'ED' (editor), a comic device borrowed from the British satirical magazine *Private Eye*. In *The Triumph of Love*, Hill deploys a more typically postmodern multiplicity of discourses and registers. At the same time he retains both his perennial preoccupations and love of devices such as paradox, oxymoron and punning. Moreover, he continues to assert the crucial importance of Christian texts and modes of understanding, suggesting in section XI that the book of Daniel offers the most adequate way to understand the destruction of modern warfare and the cruelties of Fascism.

The subtlety and complexity of Hill's poetry make any straightforward summary of its relationship to religious faith impossible. However, it may be appropriate to end this chapter by referring to the Gauguin painting *The Vision after the Sermon: Jacob Wrestling with the Angel*, a detail of which appears on the cover of Hill's *Collected Poems*.[39] The detail depicts a rather indistinct pair of wrestling figures, dressed in black, one with yellow wings, on a vivid red background. In the full painting we can see in the foreground the heads of a row of Breton women, who have presumably just emerged from church after hearing a sermon on the relevant Biblical text. In a radio broadcast, Hill spoke at length about the painting, which he said had awakened him to the power and beauty of painting (at the age of about 40), leaving him 'a changed man'. Acknowledging, but dissenting from, a view of the painting as expressing Gauguin's 'secularist condescension to the archaic pieties' (of rural Brittany), Hill argued that 'the painting which depicts a vision is itself and in its own right a vision'; and this despite Gauguin's own statement that 'I believe that the landscape and the fight exist only in the imagination of the people'. Hill's argument, in other words, is that the religious and visionary qualities of the painting are independent of Gauguin's personal beliefs, an argument which he implicitly invites us to apply to his own poetry. The apparent discrepancy between this 'powerful and generous vision' of religious faith on one hand, and Gauguin's secularist views and sometimes harsh personality on the other, supports Hill's view that an authentic work of art is not the direct product of 'the artist's authentic self'; indeed that 'in the act of making the artist may become a stranger to himself or herself'.[40] Asked on an earlier occasion whether he should be described as 'a religious poet', he answered with reference to the same painting:

> I think that the wrestling pair might actually be the village horse
> ... These village girls have come out full of ecstasy from the
> sermon, and they see what they believe they see. Gauguin paints
> them and their belief I think with great sympathy. He does not in
> any way mock that faith but he puts enough in the painting to
> imply that he himself has perhaps seen something that they have
> not, so that there is sympathy and there is detachment. (BF)

Sympathy and detachment are not, of course, simple equivalents for faith and doubt, but the duality which Hill finds in Gauguin's painting is evident in the combination of visionary and sceptical impulses in his own poetry. Hill's two comments on the picture are different in emphasis, one stressing the independence of the work of art from its creator, the other asserting the artist's ability to balance contrary impulses of admiration and scepticism. Both, though, are very relevant to his own aesthetic principles. As we have seen, such transformations of the self and balancing of contraries are crucial achievements of Hill's poetry.

Postscript: *The Orchards of Syon*

The advance publicity for *The Orchards of Syon* indicated (presumably on Hill's own authority) that it should be seen as the fourth in a series which started in 1996 with *Canaan*, so that 'read together, these four books – each a distinct and complete aesthetic achievement – form a single great poem, a kind of high-modernist *Divine Comedy* that is at once a prophetic judgment on man's fallen state and a sad and angry consolation' (the final phrase borrowed from *The Triumph of Love*, section CXLVII).[1] As has already been noted, Hill's life and work have rarely been obviously aligned, but biographical and circumstantial details would certainly accord with the idea of a break following *Collected Poems* (1985) and a new phase. Between *The Mystery of the Charity of Charles Péguy* in 1983, and the first publication in 1990 of poems later to be included in *Canaan*, Hill published little poetry, and major events transformed his circumstances: remarriage, the start of a second family, heart problems, a move from Britain to the United States, and successful treatment for long-standing depression. After a thirteen-year gap (1983–96) in new volumes of poetry, 1996–2002 has seen four volumes in six years.[2] In terms of poetic form the continuities between *The Triumph of Love* (1998), *Speech! Speech!* (2000) and *The Orchards of Syon* (2002) are immediately apparent, since each is a book-length sequence of free verse sections, whereas *Canaan* (1996) comprises short sequences and individual lyrics. *Canaan* does, however, signal a decisive move away from rhyme to free verse, rhyme having been a significant though by no mean consistent feature of

Hill's poetry up to the time of *The Mystery*. The use, in some poems from *Canaan*, of short (single phrase or single word) lines, intermittently displaced from the left-hand margin (while the devotional intensity of the language echoes earlier lyrics), seems to emphasize visually the break-up of the tight lyrical and metrical form of much of Hill's earlier work. In that sense, *Canaan* might seem to inaugurate a new phase, but not in any obvious way to begin a sequence. In terms of form, it rather figures as a transitional volume, preparing the way for the very different formal innovations of the long sequences which are to follow. In these, diction, stress and metrical marks, enjambment, allusion and self-reference generate rapid shifts in tone and meaning and sharp juxtapositions of contrasting modes, within an overall structure which combines freedom with a certain regularity (straight left-hand margins, free verse sections, of variable length in *The Triumph of Love*, but of consistent length in *Speech! Speech!* and *The Orchards of Syon*).

Thematically, it is possible to see the four volumes as linked by a vision of contemporary Britain which, if not prophetic (a problematic description, as discussed in chapter 2), is at least concerned to assess, critique, satirize and mourn. In *The Orchards of Syon*, though, the mode of satire, with its character-istic notes of mockery, condemnation and ridicule, is far less prominent and the focus is more on the emotional and intellectual contours of individual human experience. Hill himself has commented that it is 'a very different book in spirit – much more forgiving than *Speech! Speech!*'.[3] The key mode of the new volume is rather that of pastoral – like satire an ancient mode with a rich history going back to classical literature – though Hill continues to create his own late-modernist hybrid form out of multiple modes and models. Pastoral, originally concerned with the idealized life of shep-herds, crucially involves the evocation of a golden, or pre-lapsarian world and the celebration of rural beauty and harmony, though it can also involve mourning to the extent that this world is seen as lost, and can be strongly tinged with thoughts of death (as in the pastoral elegy). The Fall of Man has been crucial to Hill's imagination throughout his career and he has often invoked 'the lost kingdom of innocence and original justice', though never without precautionary scepticism and wariness about the risks of nostalgia or spurious transcendence which hover around such an idea.[4] The epigraphs to *The Orchards of Syon* all allude to moments of transcendence, inspiration, or vision, as does the cover image (D. H. Lawrence's drawing for his novel *The Rainbow*), while the title refers to the biblical City of David, Syon or Zion, a name applied in Christian writings both to the Church and to heaven. The pastoral element in the poem itself is apparent in the natural descriptions which are among the most lyrical and immediately compelling parts of the book:

> Distant flocks merge into limestone's half-light.
> The full moon, now, rears with unhastening speed,
> sketches the black ridge-end, slides thin lustre
> downward aslant its gouged and watered scree.
>
> (*OS*, sect. XIV)

Central to the pastoral strain, though, is the theme of the orchard which runs through the book. The Orchards of Syon appear as a place of lost love or happiness: 'where I left you thinking I would return' (*OS*, sect. I). They suggest paradise but also its loss and the anticipation of death: 'the heavy-bearing trees bowed towards Fall' (*OS*, sect. XXII). Structurally the orchards serve to link together allusions to various literary, theological and artistic works. They are particularly connected with Gerard Manley Hopkins's 'Goldengrove', from his poem 'Spring and Fall'.[5] Here Hopkins addresses a child grieving over the autumn fall of leaves from a grove of trees, a grief which he interprets as a prefiguration of adult grief over both death and sin:

> It is the blight man was born for,
> It is Margaret you mourn for.[6]

Hopkins's poem is a crucial intertextual presence in *The Orchards of Syon*, establishing the associations of beauty, youth and innocence, but also of time, loss, death and sin:

> the Orchards
> of Syon that are like Goldengrove
> season beyond season.
>
> (*OS*, sect. III)

Here 'beyond' is crucially ambiguous, since it might imply either repetition (the endless cycle of seasons) or transcendence (the escape from time and change).

Alongside the central symbol of the orchard, various themes and images appear and reappear throughout the poem: age and death; plants and especially the naming of plants; looking back over a long life; stress (in both psychological and metrical senses); music; despair; grace and revelation. In particular, death is a recurrent theme of the poem, from early allusions to Donne's sermon *Death's Duel* and Cocteau's film *Orphée*, to discussion of how Goldengrove might resemble 'the wood of the suicides' in Dante's *Inferno* and images of the fighting in Normandy following the World War II D-Day landings.[7] The unifying element of the poem is voice – and not the 'strange choral voice . . . as though culture itself were speaking' noted by Romana Huk in Hill's earlier work, but something both more personal and more dramatic (rather in the sense of a dramatic monologue).[8] The voice is paradoxically both intimate – a form of highly-learned interior monologue with the freedom of movement and rapid transitions characteristic of the private mind – and very public, a rhetorical discourse of persuasion, with a distinct element of performance, of a staged voice, even at times of stand-up comedy: 'Applaud, won't you, if only first time round' (*OS*, sect. VI). Both elements are present in each of Hill's latest three volumes, but *The Orchards of Syon* tends to shift the balance rather more towards the personal. One aspect of this shift is the inclusion of a number of remarks addressed to an unspecified 'you' which (rather different from the various 'others' whose role in Hill's earlier work was discussed in chapter 1) sounds like an intimate companion (see, for example, sections I, III, X, XIV), though in other cases 'you' might refer to the reader (VI, VII), or 'Albion' (VIII), or the 'spirit of difficult/ forgiveness' (IX), or some other entity or principle evoked in the poem.

In *The Orchards of Syon*, building on *The Triumph of Love* and *Speech! Speech!*, Hill's always-complex sense of subjectivity finds a new form of articulacy. In place of tense, clamped, highly condensed 'impersonal' lyrics (such as 'History as Poetry' in *King Log*), or sequences mediated through a persona, an other, or a double (such as *Mercian Hymns* or 'The Songbook of Sebastian Arrurruz'), we find an expansive long poem, governed by a fluent, confident yet ever self-doubting, ironic and reflexive voice. This voice avoids any banal 'self-expression' because it registers a reciprocity between speaking and hearing oneself speak, between that to which the self gives a form and that which gives form to the self. There are passages which resemble introspection more than anything in Hill's earlier volumes:

> My mind, as I know it, I still discover
> in this one-off temerity, arachnidous,
> abseiling into a pit, the pit a void,
> a black hole, a galaxy in denial.
>
> (*OS*, sect. LVIII)

Such lines seem to accord with Hill's avowed turn from 'the suppression of self' to 'self-knowledge and self-criticism' (*PR* 282–3); the mind is not a given to be expressed but something to be continually discovered and recognized in the poem. Otherness, the role of the voice, and the nature of lyric poetry are thematized within the poem in meditative reflections or comic pre-emptive strikes at the critic or reader:

> A radical
> otherness, as it's called, answers
> to its own voices:
>
> (*OS*, sect. XLV)

> Lyric cry lyric cry lyric cry, I'll
> give them lyric cry!
> Whose is the voice, faint, injured and ghostly,
> trapped in this cell phone, if it is not mine?
>
> (*OS*, sect. XXX)

The mind which organizes the poem is formidably learned and well-read, and the sheer range and rapidity of the allusions – ranging from the sermons of John Donne to Ealing comedy films, from the Jewish harvest festival to the topography of Lancashire and from the Latin Bible to lesser-known twentieth-century European composers, can seem daunting. In practice, however, simply identifying most of the allusions is not too difficult with access to an internet search engine. 'Reading' them – in the sense of reading the poem with an understanding of the role and implications of those allusions – is a different matter. This aspect of *The Orchards of Syon* clearly places it in the modernist traditions of Eliot and Pound, but in this instance Pound seems the more relevant figure. The famous allusions of Eliot's *The Waste Land* might be taken to imply an ideal reader who would already be familiar with these monuments of the Western cultural tradition. Pound's allusions are more maverick and abstruse; he doesn't expect the reader to know them already, though he does expect the reader to go and find out. Hill's allusions in *The Orchards of Syon* are in many cases not excessively abstruse – most readers will recognize some – but they are so various and idiosyncratic that it is hard to imagine an implied reader who would know all of them, other than Hill himself. In that sense they are personal; rather than holding the reader at arm's length, as Eliot's may seem to do, they offer a form of intimacy, even if a demanding one. At times there is a suggestion of notes taken while reading and thinking or a mock-didactic tone, a parody of learned explication:

> *Crimen* is not
> the root, *kómē* ís yr coiffure of fire,
>
> (*OS*, sect. XV)

The rapid shifting of register and context throughout the poem, which one might describe at times as free association were it not evidently highly wrought, brings one to the point where one is not surprised to find 'Donne's meta-theology' and 'A road drill' sharing the same line of poetry (*OS*, sect. XVIII). The risk with this mode of writing is that of hermeticism, not because we cannot trace the allusions, but because their importance in some cases seems to lie in what they mean to Hill himself, their place in his private intellectual and emotional world. Though the rich, learned complexity of that world rewards study and thought, it is easy for the reader to become weary of its strenuous demands. This is the more so because of the frequency of passages which seem to debate philosophical, theological or psychological points but in a highly enigmatic way because of the ambiguity and condensation of the language. Often these passages have the qualities of aphorism: short, paradoxical, suggestive, but highly resistant to logical analysis or paraphrase:

103

Mortal beauty is alienation; or not,
as I see it.

(OS, sect. XX)

Mystic
durables are not the prime good, nor
lust the sole licenser.

(OS, sect. II)

Both visual art and music are pervasive presences in *The Orchards of Syon* and are important sources of consolation. For example in section XXI John Singer Sargent's idyllic painting of a cloaked woman seated in a grassy orchard, *In the Orchard*, offers reassurance ('palliates my distress') after the speaker has apparently, through blurred vision, misinterpreted another painting ('a Venetian/ gilded interior, as it transpires') as an image of Goldengrove. Music appears in allusion to a variety of (often lesser-known) composers, but also in a striking (if rather mannered) attempt to render the rhythms of gospel singing:

> *I hear music, music in the air.* That
> Gospel? Súre that Gospel! Thát sure
> Gospel music in my head. Oh, my sole
> sister, you, little sister-my-soul,
> this mý Gospel, thís sure músic in mý head.

(OS, sect. VII)

More generally, one might say that part of the more forgiving tone of the poem to which Hill himself alluded derives from its celebration of the artistic and intellectual achievements of writers, thinkers, composers and painters whose work has been important to Hill. Art and the natural world are the two poles of Hill's more affirmative vision in this poem, neither of course pure, untroubled or untouched by suffering, loss or corruption, but offering much of what hope and joy Hill finds in the world. In the third section from the end, the poem ironically presages an upbeat ending: 'Difficult to end joyful starting from here,/ but I'll surprise us' (*OS*, sect. LXX). The concluding section, after some final clowning and word-play, ends with a deeply ambivalent account of the meaning of the poem's central image:

104

Here are the Orchards of Syon, neither wisdom
nor illusion of wisdom, not
compensation, not recompense: the Orchards
of Syon whatever harvests we bring them.

(*OS*, sect. LXXII)

Though the description is negative in its detail, characterizing
the orchards by what they do not represent, these lines seem
to strike a note of reconciliation or resignation, expressing a
humanist acceptance of the potential for both good and evil.
The Orchards of Syon may be seen as bringing to completion
both a new phase in Hill's work, beginning with *Canaan*, and
a trilogy of long, multi-section, rich, complex, technically
adventurous poems beginning with *The Triumph of Love*.
Indeed, the description of what a poem should be that Hill
offered in that volume – '*a sad and angry consolation*' (*TL*, sect.
CXLVIII) – would stand appropriately over the three volumes,
which mix those elements in differing degrees. Sadness is
predominant in *The Triumph of Love* as it mourns the tragedies
of twentieth-century history; anger represents the key note of
Speech! Speech! as it excoriates contemporary media culture;
consolation is more to the fore in *The Orchards of Syon* as it
revisits aspects of a life, and a life's work, in a mood that gives
more acknowledgement to 'that which sustains us' (*OS*, sect.
LXX).

Notes

INTRODUCTION

1. For example *The Lords of Limit: Essays on Literature and Ideas* (London: André Deutsch, 1984), 1; 'Under Judgment': interview with Blake Morrison, *The New Statesman*, 8 February 1980, 212; 'The Art of Poetry LXX', Geoffrey Hill interviewed by Carl Phillips, *The Paris Review*, 154 (Spring 2000), 277. The phrase is from Milton's tract *Of Education* (1644).
2. 'Postscript: Picturing the Word', BBC Radio 3, 18 September 1999.
3. Interview with Michael Dempsey, *Illustrated London News*, 20 August 1996, 24.
4. Geoffrey Hill, 'Letter from Oxford', *London Magazine* 1:4 (May 1954), 71–5.
5. 'The Poetry of Allen Tate', *Geste* (Leeds), 3:3 (November 1958), 8–12.
6. 'Dividing Legacies', *Agenda*, 34:2 (Summer 1996), 9–28; *Literary Imagination* 1:2 (Fall 1999), 240–55.

CHAPTER 1. IDENTITY AND OTHERNESS

1. 'Tradition and the Individual Talent', *Selected Essays*, 3rd edn (London: Faber, 1951), 21.
2. Romana Huk, 'Poetry of the Committed Individual: Jon Silkin, Tony Harrison, Geoffrey Hill and the Poets of Postwar Leeds', in James Acheson and Romana Huk (eds), *Contemporary British Poetry: Essays in Theory and Criticism* (Albany, NY: State University of New York Press, 1996), 175–219 (190).
3. *New Selected Poems 1966–1987* (London: Faber and Faber, 1990), 31, 32.
4. *The Notebooks of Samuel Taylor Coleridge*, ed. Kathleen Coburn, vol. I (Text) (London: Routledge & Kegan Paul, 1957), Serial no. 87,

Entry no. G 81. Hill quotes this aphorism in *The Lords of Limit: Essays on Literature and Ideas* (London: André Deutsch, 1984), p. 4 and his interview with Hermione Lee (*Book Four*, 2 October 1985, Channel Four television).

5. See for example Genesis 41:29–30.

6. Hill's commentary makes up much of the note on Hill's poetry in *The Penguin Book of Contemporary Verse 1918–60*, ed. Kenneth Allott, 2nd edn (Harmondsworth: Penguin, 1962), 390–93.

7. Christopher Ricks, *The Force of Poetry* (1984; repr. Oxford: Oxford University Press, 1987), 287; Gabriel Pearson, in Peter Robinson (ed.), *Geoffrey Hill: Essays on his Work* (Milton Keynes: Open University Press, 1985), 43.

8. See Donald Davie, Pound (London: Fontana, 1975), 52–6; John Espey, *Ezra Pound's Mauberley: A Study in Composition* (London: Faber and Faber, 1955).

9. For example Donald Davie, 'Fallen Language', in Davie, *With the Grain: Essays on Thomas Hardy and Modern British Poetry*, ed. Clive Wilmer (Manchester: Carcanet, 1998), 262.

10. R. K. Meiners, ' "Upon the Slippery Place"; or, In the Shit: Geoffrey Hill's Writing and the Failures of Modern Memory', in *Contemporary British Poetry*, 221–43 (227–8).

11. Ezra Pound, 'Hugh Selwyn Mauberley', *Collected Shorter Poems* (London: Faber, 1984), 187, 188.

12. See also Andrew Michael Roberts, 'Romantic Irony and the Postmodern Sublime: Geoffrey Hill and "Sebastian Arrurruz" ', in Edward Larrissy (ed.), *Romanticism and Postmodernism* (Cambridge: Cambridge University Press, 1999), 141–56.

13. References to *Mercian Hymns* are given in the form of the hymn number in roman numerals rather than page numbers; each hymn occupies one page in *Mercian Hymns* (London: André Deutsch, 1971) and in *Collected Poems* (Harmondsworth: Penguin, 1985), 105–34.

14. *Mercian Hymns*, Acknowledgments; *Collected Poems*, 201.

15. For example Heaney's poems 'Bogland' and 'North', *New Selected Poems*, 17–18, 56–7.

16. Heaney, *New Selected Poems*, 1–2.

17. Hill quotes the phrase from Father Christopher Devlin, in response to a question about the consolation of art, and suggests that 'there's a real sense in which every fine and moving poem bears witness to this lost kingdom' (*VP* 88).

18. *The Oxford English Dictionary*, 2nd edn (Oxford: Clarendon Press, 1989), cited in Hill's notes.

19. Hill's note tells us that 'quick forge' is a phrase from Shakespeare's *Henry V*, but that 'the source has no bearing on the

poem'. In Shakespeare the phrase is a metaphor for the rapid operation of thought; Hill's poem contrasts the appeal of a metaphorical forge with the physical damage wrought by a real one.

20. Paul Celan, *Selected Poems*, translated and introduced by Michael Hamburger (1988; London: Penguin, 1990), biographical summary, 1.

21. *The New Grove Dictionary of Music and Musicians*, ed. Stanley Sadie, 20 vols (London: Macmillan, 1986), vol. iv, 335.

22. Hamburger, introduction to Celan, *Selected Poems*, 22.

23. Celan, 172–3; 202–3. All translations of Celan's poetry are taken from Hamburger, which W. S. Milne suggests Hill used as a 'point of departure' (W. S. Milne, *An Introduction to Geoffrey Hill* (London: Bellew, 1998), 28).

24. Celan, 'Ice, Eden', 173.

25. John Kerrigan, ' "Knowing the Dead": For Peter Laver, 1947–83', *Essays in Criticism*, 37 (1987), 36–7. John Mole similarly suggests that *The Mystery* is 'an oblique autobiography of the spirit', in 'Expanding Elements: Recent Poetry', *Encounter*, 61:4 (December 1983), 65.

26. Grevel Lindop, 'Myth and Blood: The Poetry of Geoffrey Hill', *Critical Quarterly*, 26:1–2 (Spring – Summer 1984), 151.

27. References to *The Mystery of the Charity of Charles Péguy* are given in the form 2.1 (= section 2, stanza 1).

28. W. S. Milne, Review of *Speech! Speech!*, Agenda, 38:1–2 (Autumn 2000 – Winter 2001), 139–43 (140).

29. References to *The Triumph of Love* (Harmondsworth: Penguin, 1999) are given in the form of section numbers, using roman numerals.

30. Emerson, 'Self-Reliance', *Essays* (1st series) (London: George Routledge & Sons, 1900), 47–8.

31. *The Oxford Dictionary of the Christian Church*, ed. F. L. Cross and E. A. Livingstone (2nd edn; repr. Oxford: Oxford University Press, 1984), 194.

32. *The Complete Poems and Plays of T. S. Eliot* (London: Faber, 1969), 182. Michael Edwards, 'Quotidian Epic: Geoffrey Hill's *The Triumph of Love*', *The Yale Journal of Criticism*, 13:1 (Spring 2000), 167–76 (172).

33. *Aeneid*, Book VI, line 129.

34. See the opening lines of Dante's *Inferno* and the start of section V of 'East Coker' (*The Complete Poems and Plays of T. S. Eliot*, 182).

35. References to *Speech! Speech!* are given in the form of section numbers.

36. See Tom Paulin, 'The Case for Geoffrey Hill', review of *Geoffrey Hill: Essays on his Work*, ed. Peter Robinson, in *London Review of Books*, 4 April 1985, 13–14 (13); revised version 'A Visionary Nationalist: Geoffrey Hill', in *Minotaur: Poetry and the Nation State* (Cambridge, MA: Harvard University Press, 1992), 276–84 (277).

37. In *Speech! Speech!* Hill uses two metrical marks: a vertical line (|) to indicate a pause or caesura, and an accent mark (e.g. coúld) to indicate a stressed syllable. These are borrowed from the practice of Gerard Manley Hopkins.

38. For example, Hill alludes to a seventeenth-century comment (by Mildmay Fane, second Earl of Westmoreland) on the advantages, for a poet, of 'withdrawal from the "competitive negotium" of courtly and urban life', but adds that 'even while he is propounding a doctrine of contemplative withdrawal, the poet is necessarily engaged in a competitive *negotium*; he is competing with the strengths and resistances and enticements of the English language' (*EC* 9–10).

39. *Workers' Playtime* was a BBC 'Light Programme' radio programme of the 1940s, mentioned by Hill as a feature of his childhood (*PR* 286). 'Aunty' and '[the] Beeb' are mocking or affectionate terms for the BBC.

40. Rorke's Drift was a battle during the Zulu War of 1879 between a force of about 100 British soldiers and about 4,000 Zulus. The British force inflicted heavy losses on the Zulus and held out until a relief force appeared. The Battle of Jutland, the largest naval battle of World War I, took place in May 1916 between the German and British fleets; both sides suffered heavy losses.

41. Hill has argued that in George Eliot's 1868 political pamphlet *Address to Working Men by Felix Holt* she 'has denied us the cross-rhythms and counterpointings which ought . . . to be part of the structure of such writing . . . she has excluded the antiphonal voice of the heckler' ('Redeeming the Time', *LL* 90).

42. Geoffrey Hill, reading his poetry at the University of Salford, Friday 30 June 2000.

CHAPTER 2. HISTORY AND POLITICS

1. *Lope de Vega: Five Plays*, trans. Jill Booty, ed. R. D. F. Pring-Mill (New York: Hill and Wang, 1961), 199, note 1; R. O. Jones, *A Literary History of Spain: The Golden Age: Prose and Poetry* (London: Ernest Benn, 1971), 87–8.

2. Oastler, who campaigned for shorter hours and better conditions for mill workers, sought to develop an anti-individualist, anti-

trade form of Toryism, based on the continuity of traditional (especially rural) life, institutions and hierarchies, combined with piety and humanitarian benevolence.

3. Both views are found in Paulin, 'The Case for Geoffrey Hill'. See also John Lucas, letter to the *London Review of Books*, 3 October 1985, 4.

4. Steven Connor, *Postmodernist Culture: An Introduction to Theories of the Contemporary* (2nd edn, Oxford and Cambridge, MA: Blackwell, 1997), 124.

5. Connor, *Postmodernist Culture*, 125.

6. *Letters on Poetry from W. B. Yeats to Dorothy Wellesley* (London, 1940), 24; T. S. Eliot, *On Poetry and Poets* (London: Faber, 1957), 98; quoted in *The Lords of Limit: Essays on Literature and Ideas* (London: André Deutsch, 1984), 2.

7. *The Lords of Limit*, 9, quoting Eliot, *On Poetry and Poets*, 86–7.

8. T. S. Eliot, 'Little Gidding', *The Complete Poems and Plays of T. S. Eliot*, 197.

9. The presence of the phrase 'fat cat' was pointed out by Gabriel Pearson (*GH* 33).

10. Paulin, 'The Case for Geoffrey Hill', 13.

11. See the following letters in the *London Review of Books*: Craig Raine, 2 May 1985, 4; Martin Dodsworth, 23 May 1985, 4; Tom Paulin, 6 June 1985, 4; Craig Raine, 20 June 1985, 4; Martin Dodsworth, 18 July 1985, 4; Tom Paulin, 1 August 1985, 4; Martin Dodsworth, 5 September 1985, 4; John Lucas, 3 October 1985, 4; Eric Griffiths and Martin Dodsworth, 7 November 1985, 4; John Lucas, 5 December 1985, 4–5; Eric Griffiths, 6 February 1986, 4.

12. Letter of 6 June 1985.

13. A. Welby Pugin, *An Apology for the Revival of Christian Architecture in England* (London: John Weale, 1843), 2, 37–8.

14. *Anima Poetae: From the Unpublished Note-Books of Samuel Taylor Coleridge*, ed. Ernest Hartley Coleridge (London: Heinemann, 1895), 151. James Harrington was a seventeenth-century republican political writer.

15. Robert Blake, *Disraeli* (London: Eyre & Spottiswoode, 1966), 210.

16. John Henry Newman, *Loss and Gain: The Story of a Convert*, ed. Alan G. Hill (1848; Oxford: Oxford University Press, 1986), see 90, 143–4.

17. *Coningsby, or, the New Generation*, ed. Sheila M. Smith (Oxford: Oxford University Press, 1982), p. x.

18. Benjamin Disraeli, *Coningsby, or, the New Generation* (1844; London: Dent, 1959), book VIII, chapter III, 340.

19. 'Geoffrey Hill writes:' (about *Tenebrae*), *Poetry Book Society Bulletin*, 98 (Autumn 1978), unpaginated.

20. T. S. Eliot, 'The Function of Criticism', *Selected Essays*, 29.

21. Ronald Blythe, 'Satan without Seraphs', review of *Religion and the Decline of Magic*, by Keith Thomas, *Listener*, 4 February 1971, 150–51.

22. *London Review of Books*, Letters of 3 October 1985 and 5 December 1985, 5.

23. *London Review of Books*, Letter of 5 December 1985, 5.

24. Ibid.

25. *London Review of Books*, Letter of 6 February 1986.

26. *Old Moore's Almanac* is an annual book of predictions.

27. Karl Marx and Friedrich Engels, *The Communist Manifesto*, trans. Samuel Moore (Harmondsworth: Penguin, 1967), 83.

28. 'J'accuse!' refers to the title of Emile Zola's open letter in defence of Alfred Dreyfus, a Jewish French army office who was the victim of a famous miscarriage of justice during the 1890s; Péguy was also a 'Dreyfusard' (defender of Dreyfus).

29. See *Julius Caesar*, Act III, scene ii.

30. See for example *The Times*, 1 November 1994, 1, 8.

31. The Oxford Authors, *Andrew Marvell*, ed. Frank Kermode and Keith Walker (Oxford and New York: Oxford University Press, 1990), 95.

32. *Complete Prose Works of John Milton*, vol. ii, 1643–8, ed. Ernest Sirluck (New Haven: Yale University Press, 1959), 551.

33. *Canaan* (Harmondsworth: Penguin, 1996), vii, quoting from Zephaniah 2:5, the Geneva Bible of 1560.

34. Peter Sanger, 'Sobieski's Shield: On Geoffrey Hill's *The Enemy's Country* (1991) and *New and Collected Poems* (1994)', *Antigonish Review*, 109 (1997), 133–50 (150); Peter Firchow, review of *Canaan*, *World Literature Today*, 72 (1998), 620.

35. Harold Bloom, quoted on back cover of *Speech! Speech!*

36. Marcus Waithe, ' "Whose Jerusalem"? – Prophecy and the Problem of Destination in Geoffrey Hill's "Canaan" and "Churchill's Funeral" ', *English*, 51 (2002), 261–76 (274).

37. Sanger, 'Sobieski's Shield', 144.

38. This association arises especially from the tradition of playing and singing a tune from Elgar's *Pomp and Circumstance* march, no. 1, to the imperialistic words of 'Land of Hope and Glory', at the last night of the annual London 'Proms'.

39. William Blake, *The Complete Poems*, ed. W. H. Stevenson (London: Longman, 1971), 219, 60, 213.

40. Malcolm Bull, quoting Frank Kermode, *London Review of Books*, 9 December 1999, 9. 'Eternal City' translates the Latin *Urbs Aeterna*, a designation of Rome found in classical writers and documents,

later applied to the role of Rome in the Christian Church (*Oxford Dictionary of the Christian Church*, 472).

41. George Butterworth was killed at Pozières, during the Battle of the Somme, in 1916. Edward Thomas was killed during the Battle of Arras in 1917.

42. *Ulysses*, ed. Hans Walter Gabler (Harmondsworth: Penguin, 1986), 28.

43. Howard Caygill, 'Benjamin, Heidegger and the Destruction of Tradition', in *Walter Benjamin's Philosophy: Destruction and Experience*, ed. Andrew Benjamin and Peter Osborne (London and New York: Routledge, 1994), 10.

44. The idea of a postmodern loss of faith in 'grand narratives' (such as the Enlightenment narrative of human progress) derives from the work of Jean-François Lyotard.

CHAPTER 3. FAITH AND DOUBT

1. See, for example, Peter Robinson (ed.), *Geoffrey Hill: Essays on his Work* (Milton Keynes: Open University Press, 1985), 25; Henry Hart, *The Poetry of Geoffrey Hill* (Carbondale / Edwardsville: Southern Illinois University Press, 1986), 2; Vincent Sherry, *The Uncommon Tongue: The Poetry and Criticism of Geoffrey Hill* (Ann Arbor: University of Michigan Press, 1987), 40. John Bayley, however, argues that 'the "I" . . . is not the poet himself, or any extension of his own person' (*GH* 191).

2. The version in *For the Unfallen* (London: André Deutsch, 1959) includes a second line, omitted in *Collected Poems* (Harmondsworth: Penguin, 1985).

3. *Biographia Literaria*, ed. George Watson (London: Dent, 1975), 167. The relevance of the Primary Imagination to 'Genesis' is discussed by Ricks (*FP* 339).

4. Harold Bloom, 'Geoffrey Hill: The Survival of Strong Poetry', Introduction to Geoffrey Hill's *Somewhere is Such a Kingdom: Poems 1952–1971* (Boston: Houghton Mifflin, 1975), repr. in *Figures of Capable Imagination* (New York: Seabury Press, 1976), 234–46 (237).

5. Ad de Vries, *Dictionary of Symbols and Imagery* (rev. edn, Amsterdam: North Holland Publishing Co., 1976), 81.

6. Karl Barth, *The Epistle to the Romans*, trans. from the 5th edn by E. C. Hoskyns (London: Oxford University Press, 1933), 60, 29. Hill refers to Barth's theology in various of his prose works: see *The Lords of Limit: Essays on Literature and Ideas* (London: André Deutsch, 1984), 1, 15, 116; *A Sermon Delivered at Great St Mary's University Church*, Cambridge, 8 May 1983, 3–4.

7. Tenebrae is the 'popular name for the special form of Matins and Lauds provided for the last three days of Holy Week', including 'the ceremony of extinguishing the lights in church one by one during the service' (*The Oxford Dictionary of the Christian Church*, 1349).

8. Robert Southwell, 'Saint Peter's Complaint', in *English Recusant Literature, 1558–1640*, ed. D. M. Rogers, vol. 76, *John Falconer, 'The Mirrour of Created Perfection', 1632; Robert Southwell, 'S. Peter's Complaint and Saint Mary Magdalens Funerall Teares', 1616* (facsimile of 1616 edn) (Menston: Yorkshire, Scolar Press, 1971), 3.

9. Edmund Spenser, *Amoretti*, sonnet 14, lines 13–14, in *Elizabethan Sonnets*, ed. Maurice Evans (London: Dent, 1977), 120.

10. W. B. Yeats, letter of 25 May 1933 to Olivia Shakepear, *The Letters of W. B. Yeats*, ed. Allan Wade (London: Rupert Hart-Davis, 1954), 810; Simone Weil, *First and Last Notebooks*, trans. Richard Rees (Oxford: Oxford University Press, 1970), 284.

11. John Donne, 'A Sermon Preached to Queen Anne, At Denmark-House, 14 December 1617', *The Sermons of John Donne*, ed. George R. Potter and Evelyn M. Simpson, 10 vols. (Berkeley: University of California Press, 1953–62), vol. i, 236–51 (236).

12. Simone Weil, *Gravity and Grace*, trans. Emma Crawford (London: Routledge & Kegan Paul, 1952), 20.

13. Robert Southwell, *Marie Magdalens Funeral Teares*, 1591, 'The Epistle Dedicatory: To the Right Worthy and Vertuous Gentle-Woman, Mrs. D. A.', *English Recusant Literature*, vol. 76, 46.

14. Hill has linked this inversion to the musical device termed 'inversion'. Notes to a concert and poetry reading given in Emmanuel Old Library, Cambridge, 17 February 1982. This event, in which Hill read 'Lachrimae', 'The Pentecost Castle', 'Tenebrae' and 'Two Chorale-Preludes', interspersed between the playing of musical works by Thomas Tallis, Orlando Gibbons, John Dowland, John Jenkins and Thomas Tomkins, suggests that Hill attaches considerable importance to the close links between *Tenebrae* and Renaissance music. See also Andrew Michael Roberts, 'Variation and False Relation in Geoffrey Hill's *Tenebrae*', *Essays in Criticism* 43:2 (April 1993), 123–43.

15. Hill's idea of art as 'exemplary' (see *VP* 99) tends to draw his idea of the artist closer to the idea of the martyr. He has also talked of martyrdom in terms which bring it closer to the technique of the artist: '[amongst] the Catholic martyrs of the age of Elizabeth I, there seems to have been what I might call a pedagogy of martyrdom, a scholastic process of training towards that deliberate goal' (*VP* 90–91).

16. David Trotter, *The Making of the Reader: Language and Subjectivity in Modern American, English and Irish Poetry* (London: Macmillan, 1984), 31.
17. *The Complete Poems and Plays of T. S. Eliot*, 196.
18. 'Geoffrey Hill writes:' (about *Tenebrae*), *Poetry Book Society Bulletin*, 98 (1978), unpaginated.
19. R. O. Jones, *A Literary History of Spain: The Golden Age: Prose and Poetry* (London: Ernest Benn, 1971), 87, 88.
20. Frank Kermode, 'D. H. Lawrence and the Apocalytic Types', in *Modern Essays* (London: Fontana, 1971), 153.
21. Kermode, 'D. H. Lawrence and the Apocalyptic Types', 154.
22. For details of correspondences, see Roberts, 'Variation and False Relation in Geoffrey Hill's *Tenebrae'*. While there are some close correspondences, in other cases Hill's poems draw on the atmosphere, imagery and vocabulary of a group or series among the Spanish poems, without closely following any single one.
23. *The Penguin Book of Spanish Verse*, ed. J. M. Cohen, 3rd edn (Harmondsworth: Penguin, 1988), 133, 135, 137, 139.
24. *The New Grove Dictionary of Music and Musicians*, vol. xix, 536.
25. Dowland, *Lachrimæ or Seven Teares Figured in Seaven Passionate Pavans* (London, 1604).
26. Diana Poulton, *John Dowland* (1972; rev. edn, London: Faber and Faber, 1982), 347.
27. *The New Grove Dictionary of Music and Musicians*, vol. vi, 374–5.
28. 'Que tengo yo que mi amistad procuras?', *The Penguin Book of Spanish Verse*, 301–3.
29. Weil, *Gravity and Grace*, 28.
30. 'The Dry Salvages' V, *The Complete Poems and Plays of T. S. Eliot*, 189–90.
31. John Taylor, review of *Canaan*, *Poetry*, 172:4 (July 1998), 236.
32. See the work which Hill cites, Sears Jayne, *John Colet and Marsilio Ficino* (London: Oxford University Press, 1963), 5.
33. Trans. Sears Jayne, in *John Colet and Marsilio Ficino*, 120.
34. Ibid.
35. 'The Dry Salvages' III, *The Complete Poems and Plays of T. S. Eliot*, 187.
36. Weil, *Gravity and Grace*, 2–3.
37. See for example *The Lords of Limit: Essays on Literature and Ideas* (London: André Deutsch, 1984), 151, 194; *The Enemy's Country: Words, Contexture, and Other Circumstances of Language* (Oxford: Clarendon Press, 1991),16.
38. Weil, *Gravity and Grace*, 29.

39. The work was painted by Paul Gauguin in 1888 at Pont-Aven in Brittany and alludes to Genesis 32:24–31.
40. 'Postscript: Picturing the Word', BBC Radio 3, 18 September 1999.

POSTSCRIPT: *THE ORCHARDS OF SYON*

1. http://www.counterpointpress.com/1582431663.html. Retrieved 10 January 2002.
2. *New and Collected Poems* (1994) contained thirteen new poems or sequences, later to appear in *Canaan*.
3. Geoffrey Hill, poetry reading at Warwick Arts Centre, 22 May 2001.
4. See chapter 1, note 17 above.
5. Hopkins's continuing importance to Hill was signalled in a lecture entitled 'Writing into the Language', which he gave in May 2001 at a conference on his work at the University of Warwick.
6. Gerard Manley Hopkins, 'Spring and Fall', *Gerard Manley Hopkins* (The Oxford Authors), ed. Catherine Phillips (Oxford and New York: Oxford University Press, 1986), 152.
7. Section II of the poem mentions *Death's Duel*, a sermon preached by John Donne shortly before his own death in 1630. Section IV alludes to the film *Orphée* (1949), directed by Jean Cocteau, a retelling of the story of Orpheus and Eurydice, with Maria Casarès in the part of Death (a beautiful princess). Section XIX refers to Canto XIII of Dante's *Inferno*, portraying the section of hell reserved for those who committed suicide, and whose souls grow into thorn bushes. Section XLIV refers to 'odours of death' in the Normandy 'bocage' (a countryside of dense hedgerows).
8. See chapter 1, note 2.

Select Bibliography

WORKS BY GEOFFREY HILL

For the Unfallen (London: André Deutsch, 1959).

King Log (London: André Deutsch, 1968).

Mercian Hymns (London: André Deutsch, 1971).

Somewhere is Such a Kingdom: Poems 1952–1971 (Boston: Houghton Mifflin, 1975).

Tenebrae (London: André Deutsch, 1978).

Brand, by Henrik Ibsen: A Version for the English Stage (London: Heinemann, 1978); revised 2nd edn (Minneapolis: University of Minnesota Press, 1981); revised 3rd edn (Harmondsworth: Penguin, 1996).

The Mystery of the Charity of Charles Péguy (London: Agenda Editions and André Deutsch, 1983).

The Lords of Limit: Essays on Literature and Ideas (London: André Deutsch, 1984).

Collected Poems (Harmondsworth: Penguin, 1985; hardback edn, London: André Deutsch, 1986).

The Enemy's Country: Words, Contexture, and Other Circumstances of Language (Oxford: Clarendon Press, 1991).

New and Collected Poems (Boston and New York: Houghton Mifflin, 1994).

Canaan (Harmondsworth: Penguin, 1996; Boston: Houghton Mifflin, 2001).

The Triumph of Love (Boston and New York: Houghton Mifflin, 1998; Harmondsworth: Penguin: 1999).

Speech! Speech! (Washington, DC: Counterpoint, 2000; Harmondsworth: Penguin, 2001).

The Orchards of Syon (Washington, DC: Counterpoint; Harmondsworth: Penguin, 2002).

INTERVIEWS

Haffenden, John, *Quarto*, 15 (March 1981), 19–22, repr. in *Viewpoints: Poets in Conversation with John Haffenden* (London: Faber and Faber 1981), 76–99.

Morrison, Blake, 'Under Judgment', *New Statesman*, 8 February 1980, 212–14.

Phillips, Carl, *Paris Review*, 154 (Spring 2000), 272–99.

CRITICAL STUDIES

Books

Bloom, Harold (ed.), *Geoffrey Hill*, Modern Critical Views (New York: Chelsea House, 1985). A useful collection reprinting some classic articles on Hill, including those by Silkin (1972), Ricks (1978), Brown and Heaney (the relevant section).

Hart, Henry, *The Poetry of Geoffrey Hill* (Carbondale/ Edwardsville: Southern Illinois University Press, 1986). Discusses Hill's early uncollected poems and each of his volumes of poetry up to *The Mystery*. Useful on Hill's allusions and influences, although Hart's interpretations of poems are sometimes strained.

Knottenbelt, E. M., *Passionate Intelligence: The Poetry of Geoffrey Hill* (Amsterdam and Atlanta, GA: Rodopi, 1990). Detailed discussion of volumes up to *The Mystery*, presenting Hill's work as 'a poetry of extremes calling forth extreme reactions'.

Milne, W. S., *An Introduction to Geoffrey Hill* (London: Bellew, 1998). Covers Hill's poetry up to *Canaan*, with sections on his life, his early uncollected poems and his poetics. Makes extensive reference to Hill's own essays and offers strongly argued interpretations of the poetry. No notes or index.

Robinson, Peter (ed.), *Geoffrey Hill: Essays on his Work* (Milton Keynes: Open University Press, 1985). Chapters on Hill's early poems and each of the volumes up to *The Mystery*, as well as *Brand*, plus seven thematic chapters. Includes a bibliography of works by and about Geoffrey Hill. With contributions by a range of well-known critics, this is still the most useful single volume on Hill's work up to the mid-1980s.

Sherry, Vincent, *The Uncommon Tongue: The Poetry and Criticism of Geoffrey Hill* (Ann Arbor: University of Michigan Press, 1987). Discusses each volume of poetry up to *The Mystery*, with considerable reference to Hill's own critical works and to his influences and affinities in British and American poetry. The interpretations are generally subtler and more convincing than Hart's, although Sherry at times imposes his own scheme of ideas too much.

Articles

The following represents a selection from the very large number of articles on Hill's work. A full critical bibliography up to 1984, by Philip Horne, is included in *Geoffrey Hill: Essays on his Work* (see above).

Agenda: Geoffrey Hill Special Issue, 17:1 (Spring 1979). Six articles on *Tenebrae* and one on 'Funeral Music'. Includes a sympathetic but interestingly sceptical piece by John Bayley.

Agenda, 30:1–2 (Spring – Summer 1992), 'Geoffrey Hill Sixtieth Birthday Issue'. Sixteen mostly short pieces on specific topics, including a memoir by a school friend, Norman Rea, with poems written by Hill at school.

Agenda, 34:2 (Summer 1996), 'A Tribute to Geoffrey Hill'. Includes an article by Hill on T. S. Eliot, plus critical articles, especially on *Canaan* (notably Jeffrey Wainwright's 'History as Poetry', one of the best discussions of this volume); also a memoir and appreciation by a school fellow of Hill's, Peter Walton.

Bloom, Harold, 'Geoffrey Hill: The Survival of Strong Poetry', Introduction to Hill's *Somewhere is Such a Kingdom*, repr. in *Figures of Capable Imagination* (New York: Seabury Press, 1976), 234–46. Eccentric but compelling celebration of Hill's earlier volumes in terms of Bloom's own theories (such as the 'strong poet' who battles with tradition through tropes) and obsessions (such as the Sublime).

Brown, Merle, 'Geoffrey Hill's 'Funeral Music', in *Double Lyric: Divisiveness and Communal Creativity in Recent English Poetry* (London: Routledge & Kegan Paul, 1980), 20–72. A subtle though at times tendentious reading of the sequence in terms of polyphonic voices.

Dodsworth, Martin, 'Ted Hughes and Geoffrey Hill: An Antithesis', in Boris Ford (ed.), *The New Pelican Guide to English Literature*, 9 vols (Penguin: Harmondsworth, 1982–8), vol. viii, *The Present* (1983), 281–93. Asserts Hill's superiority over Hughes on the grounds of Hill's reconciliation of feeling and intellect.

Edwards, Michael, 'Quotidian Epic: Geoffrey Hill's *The Triumph of Love*', *Yale Journal of Criticism*, 13:1 (Spring 2000), 167–76. Eloquent close reading of the poem.

Heaney, Seamus, 'Now and in England', *Critical Inquiry*, 3 (1977), 471–88; repr. as 'Englands of the Mind', in *Preoccupations: Selected*

Prose 1968–1978 (London and Boston: Faber, 1980), 150–69. A brilliantly poetic and impressionistic discussion of Hill, Larkin and Hughes as peculiarly English poets, including fine analysis of their respective linguistic registers.

Huk, Romana, 'Poetry of the Committed Individual: Jon Silkin, Tony Harrison, Geoffrey Hill and the Poets of Postwar Leeds', in James Acheson and Romana Huk (eds.), *Contemporary British Poetry: Essays in Theory and Criticism* (Albany, NY: State University of New York Press, 1996), 175–219. Places Hill's ethical concerns and stylistic techniques in the literary-intellectual context of Leeds and in the philosopical context of thinkers such as Sartre, Adorno and George Steiner.

Meiners, R. K., ' "Upon the Slippery Place"; or, In the Shit: Geoffrey Hill's Writing and the Failures of Modern Memory', in James Acheson and Romana Huk (eds.), *Contemporary British Poetry: Essays in Theory and Criticism* (Albany, NY: State University of New York Press, 1996), 221–43. A rich, sophisticated (and therefore quite difficult) account of Hill's unique relationship to 'postmodern appropriations of the romantic-modern tradition'.

Paulin, Tom, 'The Case for Geoffrey Hill', *London Review of Books*, 4 April 1985, 13–14; revised as 'A Visionary Nationalist: Geoffrey Hill', in *Minotaur: Poetry and the Nation State* (Cambridge, MA: Harvard University Press, 1992), 276–84. Bitter attack on Hill's work, giving the negative view of his politics and technique in extreme form.

Ricks, Christopher, 'Cliché as "Responsible Speech": Geoffrey Hill', *London Magazine*, 4:8 (November 1964), 96–101; revised as 'Clichés', in *The Force of Poetry* (1984; repr. Oxford: Oxford University Press, 1987), 356–68. Influential early appreciation of Hill in terms of his 'deliberate and responsible use of cliché' as a form of 'critical self-consciousness'; compares him with Bob Dylan in this respect.

Ricks, Christopher, 'Geoffrey Hill and 'The Tongue's Atrocities', *Times Literary Supplement*, 30 June 1978; repr., with minor changes, as 'Geoffrey Hill 1: "The Tongue's Atrocities" ', in *The Force of Poetry* (1984; repr. Oxford: Oxford University Press, 1987), 285–318. A seminal discussion of Hill's 'principled distrust of the imagination', with a detailed account of the importance of parentheses in his poetry.

Roberts, Andrew Michael, 'Geoffrey Hill and Pastiche: "An Apology for the Revival of Christian Architecture in England" and *The Mystery of the Charity of Charles Peguy', Yale Journal of Criticism*, 13:1 (2000 Spring), 153–66. Assesses Hill's view of the past and treatment of cultural nostalgia through his use of pastiche.

Robinson, Alan, 'History to the Defeated: Geoffrey Hill's *The Mystery of the Charity of Charles Péguy'*, *Modern Language Review*, 82:4 (October 1987), 830–43; repr. in *Instabilities in Contemporary British Poetry* (London: Macmillan, 1988), 62–81. Reads *The Mystery* in terms of a mystification of history which Hill only partly resists.

Sanger, Peter, 'Sobieski's Shield: On Geoffrey Hill's *The Enemy's Country* (1991) and *New & Collected Poems* (1994)', *Antigonish Review*, 109 (1997), 133–50. Subtle reading of poems from *Canaan*, stressing the idea of Hill as a prophetic poet.

Silkin, Jon, 'The Poetry of Geoffrey Hill', in Michael Schmidt and Grevel Lindop (eds.), *British Poetry since 1960* (Manchester: Carcanet, 1972), 143–64. Discusses formality and the image in Hill's poetry, with sensitive readings of poems up to *Mercian Hymns*.

Trotter, David, *The Making of the Reader: Language and Subjectivity in Modern American, English and Irish Poetry* (London: Macmillan, 1984), 209–18. Concisely traces 'the pathos of origins' in Hill's first four volumes, with acute analysis of stylistic devices.

Wainwright, Jeffrey, 'Geoffrey Hill: *The Triumph of Love*', *PN Review*, 26:5 (133) May–June 2000), 13–21. Perceptive and informative reading of the poem.

Waterman, Andrew, 'The Poetry of Geoffrey Hill', in Peter Jones and Michael Schmidt (eds.), *British Poetry since 1970 – A Critical Survey* (Manchester: Carcanet, 1980), 85–102. Judicious, appreciative but at times also critical assessment of Hill's first four volumes, stressing especially links to the work of T. S. Eliot.

Index

121